BEING A CARING FATHER

THE CHRISTIAN READER BOOK ON
BEING A CARING FATHER

Edited by Ted Miller

1817

HARPER & ROW, PUBLISHERS, SAN FRANCISCO
Cambridge, Hagerstown, New York, Philadelphia
London, Mexico City, São Paulo, Sydney

 For information address Harper & Row, Publishers, Inc., 10 East 53rd Street, New York, NY 10022. Published simultaneously in Canada by Fitzhenry & Whiteside, Limited, Toronto.

Library of Congress Cataloging in Publication Data

Main entry under title:

THE CHRISTIAN READER BOOK ON BEING A CARING FATHER.

1. Fathers—Religious life—Addresses, essays, lectures. 2. Parenting—Religious aspects—Christianity—Addresses, essays, lectures. I. Miller, Ted. II. Christian reader. III. Title: Being a caring father.
BV4529.C47 1983 248.8'421 82-48421
ISBN 0-06-061384-X

---

83 84 85 86 87 10 9 8 7 6 5 4 3 2 1

COPYRIGHT ACKNOWLEDGMENTS

"The Husband Who Leads His Family" by Robert H. Schuller; from POWER IDEAS FOR A HAPPY FAMILY by Robert H. Schuller; copyright © 1972 by Robert Harold Schuller; published by Fleming H. Revell Company; reprinted by permission.

"The Glory of God's Will" by Elisabeth Elliot Leitch; from DECLARE HIS GLORY AMONG THE NATIONS, edited by David M. Howard; © 1977 by Inter-Varsity Christian Fellowship of the USA; reprinted by permission of Inter-Varsity Press, Downers Grove, Illinois 60515.

"A Gift for Your Child" by Paul Heidebrecht; originally appeared in *Moody Monthly;* reprinted by permission.

"TV Was Never This Good" by Conrad Stephens; reprinted by permission from *Power for Living,* © 1972, Scripture Press Publications, Inc., Wheaton, Illinois 60187.

"Does Your Child Know You Love Him?" by Charles Farah; from HOW TO REAR A HAPPY FAMILY, published by Moody Press, Inc.; reprinted by permission.

"Dare To Discipline" by James Dobson; from DARE TO DISCIPLINE by James Dobson; published by Tyndale House, Publishers, Inc., © 1970; reprinted by permission.

"Homes Are for Building Christians" by Howard Hendricks; originally appeared in *Moody Monthly;* reprinted by permission.

"Family Fun Can Be Done" by Mel Larson; originally appeared in *Moody Monthly;* reprinted by permission.

"Why Christian Homes Fail" by Lars I. Granberg; reprinted by permission of *The Church Herald.*

"Fathers: Fit Or Flat" by John Warder; copyright © 1974 by Campus Crusade for Christ, Inc.; reprinted by permission of *Worldwide Challenge* magazine.

"Husbands—and Happy Homes" by Lars Granberg; reprinted by permission of *ETERNITY* Magazine; copyright 1961, Evangelical Ministries, Inc., 1716 Spruce Street, Philadelphia, Pennsylvania 19103.

"Families Are For Loving" by Gladys Hunt; reprinted by permission from *Christian Life* magazine, copyright 1977, Christian Life Missions, 396 E. St. Charles Road, Wheaton, Illinois 60187.

"I Didn't Know Dad Loved Me" by Ney Bailey; from FAITH IS NOT A FEELING by Ney Bailey, copyright 1978, Here's Life Publishers, Inc.; reprinted by permission.

"Teach Your Child To Pray" by Elva Anson; reprinted from the January 1980 issue of *The Christian Herald;* used by permission of the author.

"Bringing Down the Parent-Teen Wall" by Roy B. Zuck; reprinted by permission from September 12, 1963 issue of *Baptist Herald,* Oakbrook Terrace, Illinois.

"Here's How, Fathers" by John M. Drescher; reprinted by permission of the author.

"Are You Fun To Live With?" by Bruce Larson; reprinted by permission of Faith at Work, Inc.

"Sign Up for Parenting" by Landrum R. Bolling; reprinted by permission from May 1971 issue of *Quaker Life,* 101 Quaker Hill Drive, Richmond, Indiana 47374.

"If I Had Another Chance" by John Drescher; reprinted from Evangelical Press News Service release, Box 707, La Canada, California; also appears in IF I WERE STARTING MY FAMILY AGAIN by John Drescher, Abingdon Press.

"Dad's Night at Home" by Don Crawford; reprinted from *Sunday Digest;* © 1969 by David C. Cook Publishing Co., Elgin, Illinois 60120; used by permission.

"Rags to Riches" by Robert L. Niklaus; reprinted by permission of *The Alliance Witness,* official magazine of the Christian and Missionary Alliance.

"Just a Hunk of Junk" by Lloyd Mattson; reprinted by permission from *Power for Living,* © 1972, Scripture Press Publications, Inc., Wheaton, Illinois 60187.

"The Long Dinner" by Christopher Auer; © 1981 by Christopher Auer; reprinted by permission of the author.

"How's Your Image, Dad?" by Paul Anderson; reprinted by permission from *Power for Living,* © 1974, Scripture Press Publications, Inc., Wheaton, Illinois 60187.

"When You Lose Your Job" by Brian Dyck; reprinted by permission from the October 9, 1981 issue of the *Mennonite Brethren Herald,* 159 Henderson Highway, Winnipeg, Manitoba R2L 1L4.

"My Graduation Gift" by Bernard Pearson; reprinted by permission from *The Evangelical Beacon,* magazine of the Evangelical Free Church of America; copyright © 1965.

"Fathers Can Be Beautiful!" by Marcia Schwartz; originally appeared in June 1974 issue of *Scope* (Augsburg Publishing House) under title "A Thing of Beauty"; reprinted by permission of the author.

Interior photographs by Camerique.

Contents

The Husband Who Leads His Family

by Robert H. Schuller

"I don't know what I'm doing wrong, Dr. Schuller," the distraught husband and father said to me, adding, "but I'm not getting along with my wife or my kids. I've come to the conclusion it must be my fault." After careful analysis I offered him a prescription of Eight Words of Wisdom for Husbands and Fathers.

1. *Think positively.* Think positive thoughts and positive things will happen to you.

" . . . whatever a man sows that he will also reap" (Gal. 6:7).

"Cast your bread upon the waters, for you will find it after many days" (Ecc. 11:1).

" . . . the measure you give will be the measure you get" (Matt. 7:2).

I remember a father who came in to see me because his child had gone off the deep end. He said, "I don't know what we did wrong. We taught him not to smoke and not to drink. We taught him not to swear and we taught him not to steal."

I interrupted and said, "I think that is your problem. You didn't train up the child in the way in which he *should* go. You tried to train up your child in the way in which he *should not* go." Miracles happen when positive thinking takes over.

2. *Try positively.* The positive thought must be followed, consistently, by positive effort. Too many defeated people are like the man who said: "I've got so much to do I don't know where to start, so I'll sit down first and take a rest and then that'll be done, at any rate." The truth is we generally succeed at something when we really have a burning desire to achieve. Where there's a will, there's a way.

I know too many fathers today who are trying to get ahead financially and professionally, but they are not trying with the same passion and fervor to be a success as a husband and father.

Anything worthwhile takes time, effort, and enthusiasm. There are people who are failing in daily life because they think positively but don't try with a passion.

3. *Touch tenderly*. The positive thought leads to the positive try, and the positive try leads to the positive touch.

Touching is one of our five natural senses and is consequently an enormously powerful vehicle of communication.

A father and husband who complained that "he didn't feel close to his family anymore" had a breakthrough when he followed this advice that I gave him.

"Go to your children's and to your wife's closets and touch their clothes. Then touch their faces and feel their inner life warmly vibrating through your fingertips. Also keep in close touch," I added, "on a daily basis—by contacting them by telephone and simply checking to see how they are."

This leads me to the next words of wisdom.

4. *Talk positively*. To build close relationships, keep communication lines open with time to talk positively and privately.

Be an inspiring person, not a complaining parent. Be an uplifting conversationalist, not a negative grumbler. Let your words illuminate, uplift, and amuse your household, and the mental climate will become electric with happiness. May your children grow old remembering Dad as someone who always cheered them on saying, "You can do it, son! You have the possibilities within you, and I'll help see to it that they come out!"

Create opportunities to talk privately with your wife and each of your children. I deliberately carve out of my busy schedule the occasions to be alone with my children on a personal level. I make time to pray privately with each of my children periodically. It's absolutely the most rewarding value in my life—these private times! A sensitive man will feel the need within his wife, a child, or himself for a private talk. Respond promptly and forthrightly to these feelings.

5. *Tune in positively*. Tune in and listen to what members of your family are trying or wanting to say to you. I made this resolution to my wife and children: I promise to listen when I hear you.

I remember the day I had a harsh argument with my eldest daughter, Sheila, who was a junior in high school at the time. I was rushing to get to the office and she was rushing to get to school. While I was driving her to school, I gave her an extreme verbal lashing. As I dropped her off in front of the high school, said goodbye, watched her go into the school, I noticed that she was trembling. This really bothered me. I parked my car and prayed. If you pray honestly, you begin by asking, "How can I improve myself?"

I called up the high school office and contacted the school principal, requesting, "My daughter is enrolled in your school. I must see her this noon at the lunch hour. Please grant me permission." Permission was granted.

As she came outdoors I met her with a smile, took her hand, and said, "Sheila, I certainly am not proud of the way we handled the situation—particularly the way I handled it. I want to apologize. I just don't think I acted like a Christian. There was no excuse for your behavior—but neither was there an excuse for mine. Let's go out and have lunch."

I picked out a very fine place and we had a beautiful lunch. (This was the very first time that just the two of us went out for lunch together.) Before the lunch was served, we held hands and we had a prayer. I asked God to forgive me, and he did. Sheila has told many people that she and I both felt that this was one of the most rewarding moments in our lives. We were both very honest in our explosions. We were both very honest in our confessions of missing the mark. And we were both very honest in our forgiving!

6. *Train them in positive morality.* What is morality? It is making a decision on what is *right*, not on what is *pleasurable*. The moral person never acts upon "What would I like to do?" rather on "What is the right thing to do?"

Teach your children morality and they will surely be successful persons. By necessity, this involves some powerfully positive no's!

"Follow God's example in everything you do just as a much loved child imitates his father" (Eph. 5:1 LB).

"Commit your work to the Lord, then it will succeed" (Prov. 16:3 LB).

"Train up a child in the way he should go and when he is old he will not depart from it" (Prov. 22:6).

7. *Tackle problems positively.* Practice possibility thinking as you face personal and family problems—they're bound to come! Remind

yourself—and remind your wife and children—that success is not escaping problems but facing them creatively.

Charley Boswell was a halfback and outfielder at the University of Alabama before World War II. In the European theater, on November 30, 1944, he commandeered a tank, and set out for a nearby German village and American supply depot in search of food and ammo. A German 88 shell hit the tank, setting it afire. "I got out, but I saw one of the crew was still inside. I went back, pushed him out, and just as I got out of the tank it was hit again. I woke up in the hospital blinded," Boswell said.

Months later, at Valley Forge Hospital, near Philadelphia, Corporal Kenny Gleason, a former assistant pro from Charlotte, N.C. said to Boswell, "Captain, I'm going to teach you to play golf."

Boswell recalled, "I was really depressed. How could a blind man play golf when he couldn't even see the ball? But he kept after me and I agreed. I learned to play golf."

On the course Charley just says, "Point me; I'll put the ball in the hole." And he does. Boswell is a busy man in the business world of Alabama. He has an insurance firm, an outfit that manufactures personalized golf balls, and another that makes golf gloves.

Got problems? It's possible to solve them creatively.

8. Trust positively. Now move ahead through life with a vital, happy, positive religious faith. Believe in God and live that faith. Let that faith color your whole personality, and when times seem darkest, your family will rise up and honor you. ●

The Glory of God's Will

by Elisabeth Elliot Leitch

Read 12-23-84, 11-13-92

High in the mountains of North Wales in a place called Llanymawddwy lives a shepherd named John Jones with his wife Mari and his black and white dog Mack. I stood one misty summer morning in the window of their farmhouse watching John on horseback herding the sheep with Mack. A few cows were quietly chewing their cud in a nearby corner while perhaps a hundred sheep moved across the dewy meadow toward the pens where they were to be dipped.

Mack, a champion Scottish collie, was in his glory. He came of a long line of working dogs, and he had sheep in his blood. This was what he was made for, this was what he had been trained to do, and it was a marvelous thing to see him circling to the right, circling to the left, barking, crouching, racing along, herding a stray sheep here, nipping at a stubborn one there, his eyes always glued to the sheep, his ears listening for the tiny metal whistle from his master which I couldn't hear.

Mari took me to the pens to watch what John had to do there. When all the animals had been shut inside the gates, Mack tore around the outside of the pens and took up his position at the dipping trough, frantic with expectation, waiting for the chance to leap into action again. One by one John seized the rams by their curled horns and flung them into the antiseptic. They would struggle to climb out the side, and Mack would snarl and snap at their faces to force them back in. Just as they were about to climb up the ramp at the far end John caught them by the horns with a wooden implement, spun them around, forced them under again, and held them—ears, eyes and nose submerged for a few seconds.

I've had some experiences in my life which made me feel very sympathetic to those poor rams. I couldn't figure out any reason for the treatment I was getting from the Shepherd that I trusted. And he didn't give me a hint of explanation. As I watched the struggling sheep, I thought, "If there were some way to explain! But such knowledge is too wonderful for them—it is high, they cannot attain unto it." So far as they could see, there was no point whatsoever.

When the rams had been dipped, John rode out again on his horse to herd the ewes which were in a different pasture. Again I watched with Mari as John and Mack went to work again, the one in charge, the other obedient. Sometimes, tearing at top speed around the flock, Mack would jam on four-wheeled brakes, his eyes blazing but still on the sheep, his body tense and quivering, but obedient to the command to stop. What the shepherd saw, the dog could not see—the weak ewe that lagged behind, the one caught in a bush, the danger that lay ahead for the flock.

"Do the sheep have any idea what's happening?" I asked Mari.

"Not a clue!" she said.

"And how about Mack?"

I can't forget Mari's answer:

"The dog doesn't understand the pattern—only obedience."

There are those who would call it nothing more than a conditioned reflex, or at best blind obedience. But in that Welsh pasture in the cool of that summer morning I saw far more than blind obedience. I saw two creatures who were in the fullest sense "in their glory." A man who had given his life to sheep, who loved them and loved his dog, and a dog whose trust in that man was absolute, whose obedience was instant and unconditional, and whose very meat and drink was to do the will of his master. "I delight to do thy will," was what Mack was demonstrating; "Yea, thy law is within my heart."

For Christians, the glory of God's will means absolute trust, it means the will to do his will, and it means joy.

What is this thing called trust? Did Mack's response to John's commands hinge on the dog's approval of the route his master was taking? Mack didn't know what the shepherd was up to, but he knew the shepherd. Have you and I got a Master we can trust? Do we ask first of all to be allowed to examine and approve the scheme?

The Apostle Paul admitted the limitations of his own understanding: "Now we know in part," he said; "now we see through a glass darkly." But he was absolutely sure of his Master. He never said, "I know why this is happening," but rather, "I know *whom* I have believed. I am absolutely sure that nothing can separate us from the love of God."

We start, then, with the recognition of who God is. He is our Creator, the one whose spoken word called into being the unimaginable thing called space which scientists tell us is curved, and the equally unimaginable thing called time which the Bible tells us will cease. He set the stars in their trajectories and put the sliding shutter on the lizard's eye—this is the God who dreamed you up, thought of you before light existed, created you, formed you, and now calls you by name. He says "Fear not, Susan"; he says, "I have redeemed you, Steve."

When the Apostle John was an old man in exile on the island Patmos "on account of the Word of God and the testimony of Jesus," he was granted a vision of "one like a Son of man"—eyes like a flame of fire, a voice like a waterfall, his face shining like the full strength of the sun—and in his hand he held seven stars. Old John, who had known and loved Jesus, was overwhelmed. He fell at his feet as one dead. And then the hand that held the seven stars was laid on him, and the voice that was like a thundering cataract said, "Fear not, *I am*—the first and the last; I died, I am alive, I have the keys. Now write what you see."

What John saw turned out to be the Book of the Revelation, the most abstruse of all the books of the Bible, full of bowls of wrath and bizarre beasts, of lightning and harps and smoke and seas of glass and rainbows of emerald. The courage it took to put all that down in writing for other people to read came from the vision John had had of who it was that was asking him to do it.

It is this same one who asks you and me to do what he wants us to do—the God of creation who's got the whole wide world in his hands. The God who in the person of Jesus Christ "for us men and for our salvation came down from heaven and was made man and was crucified." Those hands that kept a million worlds from spinning into oblivion were nailed motionless to a cross. For us. That hand that held the stars—laid on you. Can you trust him?

Two thousand years ago Paul said that the Jews were looking for miracles, the Greeks were seeking after wisdom. Not much has changed, has it? People are still looking for instant solutions, chasing after astrologers and gurus and therapists and counselors, but Christianity still has only one story to tell—it's an old old story: Jesus died for you; trust him.

Karl Barth was once asked to sum up in a few words all he had written in the field of theology. This was the sum: "Jesus loves me, this I know, for the Bible tells me so."

If you can trust that kind of God, what do you do next? You do what he tells you; you obey. This was the second thing I saw when I watched the shepherd and his dog. If you know your Master, you will to do his will.

This world is his show; he's running it. Do we think of it as under our management? "Do your own thing," they tell us. They even say, "If it feels good, do it." Have you ever heard a more idiotic piece of advice? Is it our world, a sort of make-your-own-sundae proposition, with the will of God just a creamy squirt of earthly success and heavenly approval that goes on top? The will of God is not something you add to your life. It's a course you choose. You either line yourself up with the Son of God and say to the Father, "Thy will be done," or you capitulate to the principle which governs the rest of the world and say, "My will be done."

Harry Blamires has said, "From the human race today goes up one mighty prayer of praise and one tremendous shout of defiance against the loving rule of God. At every moment, and in every act or thought, we swell the volume of that hymn of praise, or else of that cry of blasphemous rebellion."

We identify ourselves with Christ or we deny him. Jesus chose a path, and went down it like a thunderbolt. When we say as Christ did, "I have set my face like flint to do his will," we are baptized into his death—and like the seed which falls into the ground and dies, we rise to new life. "We have shared his death," Paul wrote to the Romans. "Let us rise and live our new lives with him. Put yourselves into God's hands as weapons of good for his own purposes."

I like that hard, clear language: *put* yourself. Obedience to God is action. I can't find anything about feelings in the Scriptures that refer to obedience. It's an act of the will—"Our wills are ours," wrote Tennyson, "to make them thine." God gave us this precious gift of freedom of the will so that we would have something to give back to him. *Put* yourself in his hands. *Choose. Give* yourself. *Present* your bodies a living sacrifice. Until you offer up your will you do not know Jesus as Lord.

There are many men and women who have said the eternal yes to God—"Thy will be done"—but still wonder how they can know what God wants them to do. They wish that God's orders were as clear as the pillar of fire to the people of Israel or the whistle's call to the shepherd dog. How can we possibly know?

Let me tell you a story. When the author of *Christ the Tiger* was a small boy he used to pull out of the cupboard the paper bags that his mother saved and spread them around the kitchen floor. This was permitted on the condition that he collect them and put them away when he finished playing. One day his mother (who also happens to be my mother) found the bags all over the kitchen and Tommy in the living room where his father was playing the piano. When she called him to pick up the bags there was a short silence. Then a small voice, "But I want to sing, 'Jesus Loves Me'." My father took the opportunity to point out that it's no good singing God's praises while you're being disobedient.

The epistle of John puts the lesson in much stronger language: "The man who claims to know God but does not obey his laws is not only a liar but lives in self-delusion."

To will to do God's will involves body, mind, and spirit, not spirit alone. Bringing the body under obedience means going to bed at a sensible hour, watching your weight, cutting out the junk food, grooming yourself carefully (for the sake of others). It means when the alarm goes off your feet hit the floor. You have to *move*.

Some of you remember hearing of Gladys Aylward, the remarkable little London parlor maid who went to China as a missionary. She spent seven years there of happy single life before an English couple came to work nearby, and as she watched them she began to realize that she had missed out on something wonderful. So she prayed that God would choose a man for her in England, call him, and send him straight out to her part of China and have him propose. As she told me the story, she leaned toward me, her bony index finger pointing in my face, and said, "Elisabeth, I believe God answers prayer; he called the man—but he never came!" It's a little like the alarm clock: the call to duty comes, but *you* have to put your feet on the floor. That's the obedience of the body.

Bringing the mind under obedience for a student means to study. Being in college puts you under a set of obligations. You must pay your tuition, go to classes, write that term paper. You don't need to pray about whether you ought to do these things.

Being a Christian puts you under certain obligations, too. You are the salt of the earth, the light of the world, and "my witnesses," Jesus said. You don't need to pray about whether this is God's will or not, but bringing your spirit under obedience entails plenty of praying for understanding and for guidance about the how, when, and where.

The Bible won't tell you whom to marry or what mission field to go to, but I believe with all my heart that as you try honestly to do the things you're sure about, God will show you the things you aren't sure about. We might as well admit that most of our difficulties are not with what we don't understand, but with what we do understand.

In preparation for writing a book on the guidance of God, I read through the whole Bible to find out how he guided people in those days. I found that in the overwhelming majority of cases it was not through what we'd call "supernatural" means—voices, visions, angels or miracles—but by natural means in the course of everyday circumstances when a man was doing what he was supposed to be doing, taking care of sheep or fighting a battle or mending fishnets.

Just before Abraham Lincoln issued the Emancipation Proclamation, a group of ministers urged him to grant immediate freedom to all slaves.

"I am approached with the most opposite opinions and advice," Lincoln wrote, "and that by religious men who are equally certain that they represent the divine will. I am sure that either the one or the other class is mistaken in that belief, and perhaps, in some respect, both. I hope it will not be irreverent for me to say that, if it is probable that God would reveal his will to others on a point so connected with my duty, it might be supposed that he would reveal it directly to me; or unless I am more deceived in myself than I often am, it is my earnest desire to know the will of Providence in this matter. And if I can learn what it is, I will do it. These are not, however, the days of miracles, and I suppose it will be granted that I am not to expect a direct revelation. I must study the plain physical facts of the case, ascertain what is possible, and learn what appears to be wise and right. The subject is difficult, and good men do not agree."

Lincoln sets for us a sane and humble example. There is no reason to assume that divine guidance is a purely spiritual matter or an inward impression. If we belong to the Lord, lock, stock, and barrel—body, mind, and spirit—why should we expect him to employ only the spirit?

If the question happens to be the matter of becoming a missionary, you have to believe that God has something to do with your even considering such a career. You may seek the advice of godly people whose wisdom you need. You look at a particular need and you may see that you could in fact fill that need. The timing may be right. You have certain gifts—gifts given for the sake of others. Circumstances may point the way. Even your own desires could be sanctified and used for God's purposes—Paul had a streak of romanticism in him, I think, when he said he wanted to preach where Christ had not been named. Why shouldn't God make use of a streak of romanticism? Study the facts. Use your head. Trust the Shepherd to show you the path of righteousness.

One week before I graduated from college, I learned that a young man named Jim Elliot was in love with me. I had been pretty sure for several months that I was in love with him, but kept telling myself that it would be fatuous to imagine that he could ever look twice at me. He was what we used to call a BTO—Big Time Operator, while I was a TWO—a Teeny Weeny Operator. Furthermore he was popular and attractive and I was sure that every little sign that he might be interested in me was only my desperately wishful thinking.

But no, he told me he loved me. My heart turned over and then sank like a stone when he went on to say that he hadn't the least inkling that God wanted him to marry me. He was going to South America, I thought I was going to Africa, and each of us had just been through months of heart searching in an attempt to accept the possibility of life as a single missionary. We believed we had reached that point, and then wham—here we were in love.

How do you discern the will of God when your own feelings shout so loud? We prayed the prayer of Whittier's hymn: "Breathe through the heats of our desire/ Thy coolness and Thy balm,/ Let sense be dumb,/ Let flesh retire,/ Speak through the earthquake, wind, and fire,/ O still voice of calm."

And one evening as we talked about what was at stake, we agreed that it really was too big for us to handle. God's call to the mission field was strong. Our love was, if anything, stronger. There seemed to be only one thing to do—put the whole thing back into the hands that were pierced for love of us, and let him do what he wanted with it. If he didn't want us together, that would be the end of it. If he did, "No good thing will he withhold from them that walk uprightly." We had to believe that promise. Some of you know the end of the story. We waited five years, then God gave us to each other for two years—does this make the will of God even more scary?

But there's a third lesson. The first, remember, as the shepherd and his dog reminded me, was that the glory of God's will for us means absolute trust; the second that it means the will to do his will; and finally it means—believe me—*joy*. It can't mean anything less from the kind of God we've been talking about.

God made us for glory and for joy. Does he ask us to offer up our wills to him so that he can destroy them? Does God take the desire of our hearts and grind it to a powder?

Be careful of your answer. Sometimes it seems that God does just that. The rams were flung helplessly into the sheep dip by the shepherd they had trusted. God led the people of Israel to a place called Marah where the water was bitter. Jesus was led into the wilderness to be tempted by the devil. The disciples were led into a storm. John the Baptist, the faithful servant, had his head chopped off at the whim of a silly dancing girl and her evil mother.

Nearly 21 years ago, five American missionaries attempted to take the gospel to a group of jungle Indians who had never heard of Christ. On the eve of their departure they sang together that great hymn by Edith Cherry:

"We rest on thee, our Shield and our Defender,
We go not forth alone against the foe.
Strong in thy strength, safe in thy keeping tender,

We rest on thee and in thy name we go."

One of the men was Jim Elliot, my husband by that time, who had written in his diary when he was a junior in college, "Father, take my life, yea, my blood if thou wilt, and consume it with thine enveloping fire. It is not mine to save; have it, Lord, pour it out for an oblation for the world."

Could Jim have imagined how literally that prayer would be answered? Months of preparation went into the effort to reach the Auca Indians of Ecuador. The men prayed, planned, worked, dropped gifts from an airplane, and believed at last that God was clearly showing them that it was time to go. They went, and they were all speared to death.

Five men who had put their trust in a God who represents himself as our Shield and our Defender were speared to death in the course of their obedience. What does that do to your faith?

A faith that disintegrates is a faith that has not rested in God himself. It rests in something less than ultimate, some neat program of how things are supposed to work, some happiness-all-the-time variety of religion. It does not recognize God as sovereign in the world and in the believer's life.

Have you forgotten that we're told to give up all right to ourselves, lose our lives for his sake, present our bodies as a living sacrifice. The word is *sacrifice*. In one of Jim's love letters—and his were different from most, I can assure you—he reminded me that if we were the sheep of his pasture we were headed for the *altar*.

But that isn't the end of the story! To get back to the question as to whether God grinds our hopes to powder, the will of God is *love*. And the love of God is not a sentiment in the divine mind, it's a purpose for the world. It's a sovereign and eternal purpose for every individual life. We follow the One who said, "My yoke is easy," yet his own pathway led straight to the cross. If we follow him, sooner or later we must encounter that cross.

So how can we say that the will of God leads to joy? We can't possibly say it unless we look beyond the cross—"For the *joy* that was set before him, Jesus endured the cross."

"Everything that happens," says Romans 8:28, "fits into a pattern for good." There is an overall pattern. When my second husband was a boy he always visualized God sitting up there surveying a huge chart. He got this idea from the Lord's Prayer: "Our Father 'chart' in heaven."

Last year my daughter and I had tea with Corrie ten Boom. As she talked about her own experience and that of my husband Jim, she took out a piece of embroidery which she held up with the back to us—just a jumble of threads that made no sense at all. She repeated for us this poem which many of you have heard:

"My life is but a weaving betwixt my God and me,
I do not choose the colors, he worketh steadily.
Oftimes he weaveth sorrow, and I in foolish pride
Forget he sees the upper and I the underside."

She then turned the piece over and we saw that it was a gold crown on a purple background.

The shepherd dog doesn't understand the pattern—only obedience. As George McDonald put it, "Obedience is but the other side of the creative will."

The will of God means joy because it is redemptive and it transforms. It is redemptive for it means joy not only for me as an individual but for the rest of the world as well. Did it ever occur to you that by your being obedient to God you are participating with Christ in his death, and then in his redemptive work?

Paul told us this. He said in the verse I quoted earlier, "We have shared his death . . . we are weapons of good for his own purposes." Your response helps all the rest of us. Obey God, I say to you, for his sake first of all. Obey him also for your own sake, for if you lose your life he promised you'd find it. And obey him too for my sake—for the sake of all of us.

There is a spiritual principle here, the same one that went into operation when Jesus went to the cross. It is the principle of the corn of wheat. The offering up of ourselves, our bodies, our wills, our plans, our deepest heart's desire to God is the laying down of our lives for the life of the world. This is the mystery of sacrifice. There is no calculating where it will end. This is what I mean by transformation.

The bitter water, the wilderness, the storm, the cross—all are changed to sweetness, peace, and life out of death. God wills to transform loss into gain, all shadow into radiance. I know he wants to give you beauty for ashes. He's given me the oil of joy for mourning, the garment of praise for the spirit of heaviness.

Jim Elliot and his four companions believed that the world and its lust pass away, but he that doeth the will of God abideth forever. Another translation says they are "part of the Permanent and cannot die." In Jim's own words, by giving up what he couldn't keep, he gained what he couldn't lose.

Because of Corrie ten Boom's obedience and that of her family through the hideousness of a concentration camp, because they looked not at what's visible but at what's invisible, hundreds of thousands have seen the light of the knowledge of the glory of God. Jesus had to go down into death; the corn of wheat had to be buried and abide alone in order to bring forth life.

The glory of God's will means trust, it means the will to do his will, and it means joy. Can you lose? Certainly you can lose your life—that's how you find it! "My life," Jesus said, "for the life of the world." What's your life for?

A Gift for Your Child

by Paul Heidebrecht

Raising a child is delicate business. A parent can unknowingly leave a child with wounds he will carry all his life. On the other hand, a parent can bless him by letting him know he is loved, important, and respected as a unique person.

This gift often not given is self-esteem. It's a healthy appreciation for oneself and self-confidence to succeed or cope with failure. It's a child accepting himself the way God made him.

Many children develop a sense of inferiority that haunts them the rest of their lives. They grow up in homes plagued with unfulfilled relationships and personal frustrations.

In his study of 7,000 young people who grew up in church-attending families, Merton Strommen discovered that one in five of the youths suffered from a low self-image. They had no sense of personal worth, lacked self-confidence, and were distressed by personal faults. They had trouble in school with students or teachers, felt alienated from God, didn't relate intimately with their parents, and worried about their relationships with the opposite sex. In a word, they were lonely.

From these lonely youths come teenage suicides and juvenile crimes. Violent behavior against themselves or others is one way of coping with their feelings of inferiority, says Strommen.

Fortunately, the majority of young people do not fall into this category. Strommen discovered that 20 percent were at the other end of the spectrum. They enjoyed being who they were and wanted to grow personally. They had good relationships and were involved with others.

The rest were somewhere in the middle. They experienced varying degrees of negative feelings about themselves. Some struggled more than others. They weren't free from a low self-image, but could be helped.

Parents can help, especially fathers. As the leaders in the home, fathers play a crucial role in developing self-confidence and a positive self-image in children.

The most important factor in developing a child's self-image is how he is treated by his parents during his first years. In her book, *Your Child's Self-Esteem*, Dorothy Briggs says that by age five a child develops his estimate of his worth. This estimate is based on the actions, statements, and expectations of his parents.

More than ten years ago, psychologist Stanley Coopersmith studied middle-class boys and their families from pre-adolescence through young adulthood. He divided the boys into two groups—those with self-esteem and those with a low self-image.

The boys with self-esteem had parents who loved them and accepted them. They were allowed to express their opinions and participate as equals in family conversations. Discipline in their homes was strict, but fair. Punishment didn't connote a loss of love.

The boys with a low self-image had parents who didn't show love and appreciation. There was little discipline, which communicated a lack of care and interest. The boys' opinions were not respected.

During his first years, a child looks to his father. The father balances the strengths and weaknesses of the mother. As the leader, he carries the major responsibility for discipline. His opinions and behavior help the child decide how he feels about himself.

Brothers and sisters also play a role in forming a child's self-image. Sensitive parents will watch their children's relationship to one another and help them show love to each other. This is especially important when the children are only a year or two apart. The younger often lives in the shadow of the older.

In his book *Hide or Seek*, James Dobson attacks two values he claims have infiltrated American society and the home. He says that beauty and intelligence are standards wrongly used to evaluate human worth. What about the child who is ugly or who is a slow learner? What is he supposed to think about himself? In far too many cases, he is made to feel inferior and rarely develops his full potential.

As a child grows with a feeling of inferiority, he gets caught in a vicious cycle where bad experiences confirm his poor image of himself. The cycle can be broken, but it isn't easy.

A factor in Christian homes is the father's theology. He may feel that putting oneself down is a sign of humility and spirituality. Man is a sinner, but he is also created in God's image, and in Christ he is a new creature.

The Christian father, by his example, must show his children that God is a loving Father. Children must be able to relate to God's mercy and kindness to appreciate themselves as God's creation.

To overlook God's justice and righteousness, however, is equally dangerous. It's important for children to understand that God's standards are best and that straying from them brings tragic consequences. When a child receives Christ, parents must show him that following Jesus helps him handle adversity and enjoy being himself.

The following list may be helpful to parents who want to build self-esteem in their children.

1. Husbands, make your relationship with your wife most important. Parents who first love each other provide security for their children.

2. Evaluate your expectations of your children. Are you requiring too much? Are you forcing them into roles they aren't ready for (e.g., Little League star, exceptional student)?

3. Examine your own self-image. Recognize your strengths and build on them. Be realistic about your weaknesses. Don't be afraid to confess weaknesses and mistakes to your children.

4. Give your children responsibilities around the home. Compliment them when they do them well. Add more responsibilities as they grow older to encourage feelings of independence and accomplishment.

5. Spend plenty of time with your children. This alone communicates that they are important to you. Involve them in your activities. For example, take them to work with you sometime, if feasible.

6. Be interested in what your children accomplish. Give lots of sincere recognition and praise.

7. Help them be realistic about their failings. Always look for areas where they succeed.

8. Show trust. Let them know you are counting on them to do certain things within their capabilities.

9. Treat them with respect. Let them express themselves and listen.

10. Prepare them for adolescence. Let them know what will happen, physically and socially, when they become teenagers.

11. Pray with your children. Thank God for each child's special gifts and abilities. ●

TV Was Never This Good

by Conrad Stephens

"I am so bored I could scream. This is absolutely the longest, most miserable evening I can remember," my wife fretted, wringing her hands and pacing back and forth from the living room to the kitchen. Our television set had been officially pronounced dead by the repairman at 1:20 that Tuesday afternoon.

Our four-year-old son first noticed the oncoming catastrophe Saturday morning when the cartoons he was watching began to brighten and dim. Sunday it was worse, and by mid-day Monday there was no picture at all.

The set had served us well for three years. An aunt had given it to us when she had bought a new color set for herself. In those three years we had been socked with only one repair bill, which came to a measly $9.90. We hoped we would get by as cheaply this time.

The repairman arrived just as we were finishing lunch dishes on Tuesday. With bated breath we awaited his diagnosis, hoping for the best and consoling ourselves that we only had $9.90 invested, should the familiar friend be beyond repair.

The repairman slowly put away his tools and tube tester (he charged by the hour), pushed the set back against the wall, stretched his shoulders, and in a most unfeeling way told us the worst. "Everything else looks O.K. Must be the picture tube. Unless this old cabinet is worth at least 40 bucks to you, I would advise you to junk it."

Whether we thought it worth $40 or not, repairing the set was out of the question. We didn't have the money, and on our tight budget we wouldn't have it for some time.

It was miserably boring and lonesome that first Tuesday evening. By 8 o'clock we had hopped into the car for the 25-mile trip to

Mother's. When we arrived at 8:30, we were greeted by my teenage brother: "Shhh. Quiet. Sit down; you're disturbing my program."

Wednesday night we went to prayer meeting at church, but the house seemed awfully empty and quiet after we returned home.

Man, you just don't realize how addicted to that electronic marvel you can get! Lots of nights I had lain down on the couch in front of the tube as early as 6 P.M. and stayed there until "Daily Prayer" at 1 A.M., getting up only for an occasional morsel of food during station breaks. Much more often I had tuned in to watch just one special program at 7 or 8, only to keep watching whatever happened to come on until the 11 o'clock news.

But we hadn't always had television. What had we done before Auntie gave us the wondrous gift? I never remembered being *this* lost for something to do.

It's been a few weeks now, and at this writing our television is still shrouded in mute darkness. We could have afforded to have it fixed by now, or even have gotten a new color set on credit. Someday we may get that color set; right now, however, we are having too much fun without it.

We have a big front porch at our house. It had been a long time since I spent a summer evening sitting there in a lawn chair, talking with the neighbors and contemplating the cloud patterns.

It had been too long since I lingered an hour after sunset to witness the birth of a summer evening, heralded by the stereo refrain of crickets and harmonizing katydids—since I listened to the children's laughter as they chase the hovering fireflies—since I caught a glimpse of the little brown bat interrupting the moths gathering about the street light—since I smelled the aroma of the night as the dew falls—since I felt the awe of standing under God's majestic Milky Way.

We spent most of our summer evenings that way when I was a kid. I had almost forgotten.

I had also forgotten how much fun it is to spend an evening cracking walnuts and mixing them into a batch of buttery fudge.

My wife and I are getting reacquainted. Before we blew the tube, most of our conversation had been during commercials. At that rate, I could have been living with a stranger in another couple of years.

We are also relearning the pleasant art of reading. I'm averaging better than one book a week now. And would you believe that both my wife and I have practically read the New Testament through since the repairman pronounced old one-eye dead?

Our conscience forced us to try having a daily Bible reading before, but it was usually a random psalm. A short psalm doesn't take long. Last night we read the entire book of 1 Corinthians—read some of it twice; we had an interesting discussion too, just my wife and I.

Family devotions aren't as hurried now either, and they are a lot more regular. Sometimes we do more than just say our prayers. We have found time to actually worship God together in our home. I have also noticed that a certain four-year-old boy sings more of his Sunday School songs and fewer TV jingles lately.

We had subscribed to a couple of church magazines, really out of loyalty more than anything else. Now we are reading them and wondering why we seldom took the time to do so before. They are terrific.

Television was never this good. But one day I know that we will get another one, and if we are not very, very careful, we will once again allow it to be a dictator in our home. I really hope not, and, dear God, if you see our new set getting the upper hand, please, blow our tube, before we blow our minds. ●

Does Your Child Know You Love Him?

by Charles Farah

Read 12-23-84

The saying, "the world is dying for a little bit of love," is equally true of many Christian homes. This is a totally unnecessary tragedy.

The Scriptures teach us "to be kindly affectioned one towards another" (Rom. 12:10). Paul, prophesying about our day, warns us that some will lack natural affection (II Tim. 3:3).

What does he mean? May we not assume that he is talking about those who, in these last days, show affection for their dogs, cats and parrots at the expense of their children?

Can we not understand that this refers to those who have been taught by our modern psychologists that a baby is to be left in the crib to cry its heart out? Not only babies, but older children as well, are literally starving for a little fondling affection from their parents. They fuss; they act ugly. They fume and sometimes break a dish or brother's balloon in order to attract attention and to tell Mom and Pop, "You owe me affection which you are not bestowing on me."

Without natural affection! What an indictment of this age! We see all about us young couples who delegate the bringing up of their children to nurses and baby-sitters. They have no time for such incidentals as bringing up a baby. However, contrary to modern thought, the proper bringing up of children is the most important function of a parent. It is not a light matter.

The dictionary defines affection as being a warm and tender attachment; fondness; love. It is not sufficient to tacitly love your children. Neither is it sufficient to think that because you provide them with a home, food and clothing that you have fulfilled your responsibility as a parent. A child *needs affection*. He needs to know that Dad and Mom love him. Nothing can substitute.

Affection-starved children do not make the best Christians nor the best citizens. They have already developed a complex that some-

times persists with them through life. They usually have a feeling that the world owes them something.

A young girl who once attended high school with our girls and who professed Christ in one of my wife's Bible classes was starved for a little affection. In an attempt to get it she would do anything from standing on her head to climbing a telephone pole. Although she was quite brilliant and capable, yet, because of the feeling that she was not wanted, at times she became sulky, unmanageable, undisciplined.

A little affection has won many a youngster to the Lord Jesus Christ. Our son David told us of an experience he had directing a boys' camp in New York State. One of the boys was unruly and disobedient and was constantly acting up. He had no respect for authority and would do all he could to make it miserable for those around him.

Finally, in desperation, David put his strong arms around the boy and told him that he loved him for Jesus' sake. The child broke down; his haughtiness disappeared instantly. They both fell to their knees. The boy surrendered to Jesus Christ.

The boy's mother wrote a beautiful letter to David which he still has in his possession. She recounts her experiences with the child before he went to camp and goes on to tell of the marvelous change that has occurred in his life since. A little affection demonstrated did what all the laws and regulations could never do.

Paul says to "teach the young women . . . to love their children" (Titus 2:4). This was in the day when Rome ruled with a rod of iron. Love was misplaced sentimentality; children were to be brought up hard, ruthless, despising the finer virtues so freely propagated by Christianity.

The exhortation to love our children is of the Lord. It is His command. This is a part of Christian doctrine, and the responsibility of young mothers.

What applies to young mothers applies equally to fathers. There are few things that a growing boy or girl appreciates more than affection from the father. God loved (I John 4:8,16). God gave (John 3:16). You are children of God—therefore, love. Love your children. Tell them you love them. Demonstration of affection by the parents generates confidence and builds up Godlike character.

One evening we were invited to dinner at the home of a couple from our church. As is customary, we sat down to visit after the repast. The wife, who is now past middle age, and who has both children and grandchildren, asked if we knew of a book on psychology that would help her overcome her troubles and difficulties. I asked for more specific information.

The story goes back to her childhood days.

During her tender childhood years and through her all-important teen years she had no affection, no love, no one who cared. She told me that the only kind or affectionate words she had ever heard came from the young man whom she married.

Although she is a fine Christian woman and has two children in the ministry, yet she still has an inferiority complex that torments her day and night. She is uncomfortable in the congregation, does not like to meet people, has times of agonizing depression and is miserable most of the time. This is by no means a singular case.

Don't deprive your children of their God-given prerogative and heritage, especially when that which you give returns to you multifold both now and in later years. Let us truly love our children and tell them about it both by act and word. ●

Dare to Discipline by Dr. James Dobson

Perhaps the most common parental error during the past twenty-five years has been related to the widespread belief that "love is enough" in raising children. Every good and worthwhile virtue was expected to bubble forth from this spring of loving kindness. As time has shown, that was wishful thinking. Although love is essential to human life, parental responsibility extends far beyond it. A parent may love a child immeasurably, and then proceed to teach him harmful attitudes. Love in the absence of proper instruction will not produce a child with self-discipline, self-control, and respect for his fellow man. Affection and warmth underlie all mental and physical health, yet they do not eliminate the need for careful training and guidance.

At a recent psychologists' conference in Los Angeles, the keynote speaker made the statement that *the greatest social disaster of this century is the belief that abundant love makes discipline unnecessary.* He said that some of the little terrors who are unmanageable in the school classroom are mistakenly believed to have emotional problems. They are referred to the school psychologist for his evaluation of their difficulty, but no deep problems are found. Instead, it becomes obvious that the children have simply never been required to inhibit their behavior or restrict their impulses. Some of these children came from homes where love was almost limitless.

Every parent should know that respectful and responsible children result from families where the proper combination of *love and discipline* is present. Both these ingredients must be applied in the necessary quantities. An absence of either is often disastrous. During the 1950's, an unfortunate imbalance existed, when we saw the predominance of a happy theory called "permissive democracy." This philosophy minimized parental obligations to control their chil-

dren, in some cases making mom and dad feel that all forms of punishment and control were harmful and unfair. As a result, the mid-century decade has been described as the most permissive ten years in our history.

Is it merely coincidental that the generation raised during that era has grown up to challenge every form of authority that confronts it? I think not. In our noble attempts to avoid the obvious hazards of authoritarian rigidity in our homes, we have run headlong into another danger of equal proportion. Certainly, other factors have contributed to the present unsettled youth scene, but I believe the major cause has been related to the anarchy that existed in millions of American homes.

Have you considered the fact that the present generation of young people has enjoyed more of the "good life" than any comparable group in the history of the world? One can define the good life any way he chooses; the conclusion remains the same. Our children have had more pleasure and entertainment, better food, more leisure time, better education, better medicine, more material goods, and more opportunities than has ever been known before. Yet they have been described as the "angry generation." How can this be? Those two conditions do not seem to fit together.

Without meaning to oversimplify a very complicated picture, it is accurate to say that many of our difficulties with the present generation of young people began in the tender years of their childhood. Little children are exceedingly vulnerable to the teaching (good or bad) of their guardians, and mistakes made in the early years prove costly, indeed. There is a critical period during the first four or five years of a child's life when he can be taught proper attitudes. These early concepts become rather permanent. When the opportunity of those years is missed, however, the prime receptivity usually vanishes, never to return.

If it is desirable that children be kind, appreciative, and pleasant, those qualities should be taught—not hoped for. If we want to see honesty, truthfulness, and unselfishness in our offspring, then these characteristics should be the conscious objectives of our early instructional process. If it is important to produce respectful, responsible young citizens, then we should set out to mold them accordingly. The point should be obvious: *heredity does not equip a child with proper attitudes; children will learn what they are taught.* We cannot expect the desirable attitudes and behavior to appear if we have not done our early homework. It seems clear that many of the parents of the post-war crop of American babies failed in that critical assignment.

Methods and philosophies regarding control of children have been the subject of heated debate and disagreement for centuries. The pendulum of social opinion has swept back and forth regularly between parental severity and the unstructured permissiveness we are witnessing today. It is time that we realize that *both* extremes leave their characteristic scars on the lives of young victims, and I would be hard pressed to say which is more damaging. When Dr. Spock and his permissive contemporaries write about the dangers of harsh, oppressive, unloving discipline, their warnings have some validity and should be heeded. However, the consequences of excessive punishment have been cited as justification for the elimination of authority and discipline. That is foolish.

There are times when a stiff-necked child will clench his little fists and dare his parent to accept his challenge; he is not motivated by frustration or inner hostility, as is often supposed. He merely wants to know where the boundaries lie and who's available to enforce them. Many well-meaning specialists have waved the banner of tolerance, but offered no solution for defiance. They have stressed the importance of parental understanding of the child, and I concur, but we need to teach junior that he has a few things to learn about mamma, too.

Respect is the fundamental ingredient in discipline and control. It is most important that a child respect his parents, not for the purpose of satisfying their egos, but because the child's relationship with his parents provides the basis for his attitude toward all other people. His view of parental authority becomes the cornerstone of his later outlook on school authority, police and law, the people with whom he will eventually live and work, and on society in general.

Respect for the parent must be maintained for another equally important reason. If you want your child to accept your values when he reaches his teen years, then you must be worthy of his respect during his younger days. When a child can successfully defy his parents during his first fifteen years, laughing in their faces and stubbornly flouting their authority, he develops a natural contempt for them.

"Stupid old Mom and Dad! I've got them wound around my little finger. Sure they love me, but I really think they're afraid of me." A child may not utter these words, but he feels them each time he outsmarts his adult companions and wins the confrontations and battles. Later he is likely to demonstrate his disrepect in a more open manner. His parents are not deserving of his respect, and he does not want to identify with anything they represent. He rejects every vestige of their philosophy. This factor is vitally important for Christian parents who wish to sell their concept of God to their children. They must first sell themselves. If they are not worthy of respect, then neither is their religion, or their morals, or their government, or their country, or any of their values. This becomes the "generation gap" at its most basic level.

Despite the popular notion to the contrary, the generation gap does not develop from our failure to communicate with our children; we're speaking approximately the same language. Mark Twain once said about the Bible, "It's not the things I don't understand that bother me; it's the things I do!" Likewise, our difficulties between generations result more from what we *do* understand in our communication than in our confusion with words. The conflict between generations occurs because of a breakdown in mutual respect, and it bears many painful consequences. What more appropriate expression of disrespect could there be than the youthful rejection of all parental values?

The issue of respect can be a useful tool in knowing when to punish and how excited one should get about a given behavior. First, the parent should decide whether an undesirable behavior represents a direct challenge of his authority—to his position as the father or mother. Punishment should depend on that evaluation. For example, suppose little Walter is acting silly in the living room, and he falls into a table, breaking many expensive china cups and other trinkets. Or suppose he loses his bicycle or leaves Dad's best saw out in the rain. These are acts of childish irresponsibility and should be handled as such. Perhaps the parent should have the child work to pay for the losses—depending on the age and maturity of the child, of course. However, these examples do not constitute direct challenges to authority. They do not emanate from willful, haughty disobedience.

In my opinion, spanking should be reserved for the moment a child (age ten or less) expresses a defiant "I will not!" or "You shut up!" When a youngster tries this kind of open rebellion, his parent had better deal with it, and minor pain is a marvelous purifier. When nose-to-nose confrontation occurs between you and your child, it is not the time to have a discussion about the virtues of obedience. It is not the occasion to send him to his room to pout. It is not appropriate to wait until poor, tired old dad comes plodding in from work, just in time to handle the conflicts of the day. You have drawn a line in the dirt, and the child has deliberately flopped his hairy little toe across it. Who is going to win? Who has the most courage? Who is in charge here? If you do not answer these questions conclusively for the child, he will precipitate other battles designed to ask them again and again. It is the ultimate paradox of childhood that a youngster wants to be controlled, but he insists that his parents earn the right to control him.

When a parent loses the early confrontations with the child, the later conflicts become harder to win. The parent who never wins, who is too weak or too tired or too busy to win, is making a costly mistake that will come back to haunt him during the child's adolescence. If you can't make a five-year-old pick up his toys, it is unlikely that you will exercise any impressive degree of control during his adolescence, the most defiant time of life. It is important to understand that adolescence is a condensation or composite of all the training and behavior that has gone before. Any unsettled matter in the first 12 years is likely to fester and erupt during adolescence. The proper time to begin disarming the teenage time-bomb is 12 years before it arrives.

Perhaps the most difficult problems referred to me occur with the rebellious, hostile teenager with whom the parents have done everything wrong since he was born. He hates them and they do not know why, because they love him thoroughly. Since adolescence is the age of natural rebellion, antagonism is added to antagonism. His relationship with his parents has long since reached a solidified stage where change is unlikely. For a psychologist, this problem must be approached as a physician views terminal cancer: "I can't cure it now; it's too late. Perhaps I can make its consequences less painful."

Lest I be misunderstood, I shall emphasize my message by stating its opposite. I am not recommending that your home be harsh and oppressive. I am not suggesting that you give your children a spanking every morning with their ham and eggs, or that you make your boys sit in the living room with their hands folded and their legs crossed. (Children are like clocks; they must be allowed to run.) I am not proposing that you try to make adults out of your little children so you can impress your adult friends with your parental skill, or that you punish your children whimsically, swinging and screaming when they don't know they have done wrong. I am not suggesting that you insulate your dignity and authority by being cold and unapproachable. These parental tactics do not produce healthy, responsible children.

By contrast, I am recommending a simple principle: when you are defiantly challenged, win decisively.

When the child asks "Who's in charge?" tell him. When he mutters, "Who loves me?" take him in your arms and surround him with affection. Treat him with respect and dignity, and expect the same from him. Then begin to enjoy the sweet benefits of competent parenthood.

Despite the current attacks on the family in our society, the concepts of marriage and parenthood were not human inventions. God, in his infinite wisdom, created and ordained the family as the basic unit of procreation and companionship. The solutions to the problems of modern parenthood can be found through the power of prayer and personal appeal to the Great Creator. Even the principles of discipline which I have summarized can hardly be considered new ideas.

Parental control with love was first recommended in the Scripture, dating back at least 2000 years.

When properly applied, discipline works! It permits the tender affection made possible by *mutual* respect between a parent and child.

It bridges the generation gap which otherwise separates family members who should love and trust each other. It allows the God of our fathers to be introduced to our beloved children. It permits a teacher to do the kind of job in the classroom for which she is commissioned. It encourages a child to respect his fellowman, and live as a responsible, constructive citizen.

As might be expected, there is a price tag on these benefits: they require courage, consistency, conviction, diligence, and enthusiastic effort. In short, one must *dare to discipline*. ●

Homes Are for Building Christians

by Howard Hendricks

Read 12-19-84

The greatest force in the life of a child, with no second competitor, is his home. A leading U. S. university spent a quarter of a million dollars to firmly establish this fact.

This is approximately how the child's waking time is divided: The public school has him 16 percent of his time; the church, 1 percent (if he is consistent in his attendance); the home 83 percent of his time.

When I was a young, naive pastor, a woman came to me one day and said, "Pastor, I want you to know that every time you open the doors of this church, I'll have my children here."

First I was elated; then I realized she was taking the responsibility God placed at her doorstep and dumping it at the doorstep of the church, saying, "Here, you take my child. You lead him to Christ. You teach him the Word of God. You be responsible for his spiritual growth and welfare."

God has given primary responsibility to teach and train the child in the Word of God to the home. This is because it is the place you can best teach truth in life terms.

In our community we have a couple who sold their business to enter vocational Christian work. Things got rough; finally they were in desperate need of food and clothing. One night at family worship, little Timmy, after Mother asked if there were any requests, said, "Mommy, do you think Jesus would mind if I asked for a shirt?"

She wrote down "shirt for Timmy" in the little book where they recorded requests and answers, and added "size 7." So every night . . . "Don't forget, Mommy, pray for the shirt." And every night they did.

One day as the mother was working around the house, she got a telephone call from a clothier in downtown Dallas. "I am just completing our July clearance sale," he said, "and I've got some shirts left over. You've got four boys; it occurred to me that you might be able to use some."

"What size?" she asked.

"Size 7."

"How many?"

"Twelve. Could you use them?"

Most of us in this position would have taken the shirts, stuffed them in the bureau drawer, made some casual comment to the child and that would be it. Not this wise parent. That night, as she expected, little Timmy said, "Mommy, don't forget the shirt; gotta pray for that."

"No, Timmy," she said, "we can thank the Lord; He answered our prayer."

"He did?"

Little Timmy's eyes went wide. As previously arranged, Tommy, the older boy, went out, got a shirt, brought it in and put it down on the table. He went out, got another shirt and brought it back. Out and back—twelve times! One little boy in Dallas believes there is a God in heaven interested enough in a boy's needs to supply a shirt.

God daily supplies golden opportunities to parents sensitive to see His working, to convey living truth in terms of life. That's why Moses said to the people that they were to teach their children with diligence, that they were to talk about the Word of God in their homes the first thing in the morning and the last thing at night. "No matter what you are doing," it is implied, "I will arrange for you opportunities to demonstrate truth in daily life."

Now, let me spell out a few essentials for developing genuine Christian living in your home.

First of all, the child must come to a saving knowledge of Jesus Christ before he ever can know anything of the dynamic power of God in his life. We need to comfort our children with the Gospel of the grace of God. Many a child, brought up in a Christian home, never makes a profession of faith nor has a real experience with Jesus Christ. Often we take it for granted he has. A young man grew up in a Christian home, attended a Christian college, came to the seminary where I teach, graduated and was three years into the ministry when he actually trusted Christ as his Saviour!

To expect a child to live the Christian life when he does not possess that life is to ask him to fly when he has no wings. The Christian life is a supernatural life. It demands supernatural power in the person of the Spirit. But it's amazing how frequently we ignore this basic fact.

To lead others to Christ without reaching one's children is not unusual. But I could think of nothing more tragic than coming to the presence of God in eternity only to discover that my children were absent because of my neglect. The greatest thrill of my life was leading three of my four children to a knowledge of Jesus Christ as Saviour; my wife led the fourth to Him. Can you think of anything more rewarding from an eternal vantage point?

The second essential for communicating truths is to develop a bond of Christian love and rapport with your children. When is the last time you told your children you love them? Did you ever pick that kid right up off the floor, cover him with kisses and say, "Buddy, I love you more than life. And I always will love you, pal, no matter what happens. I'm on your team"?

I go into many homes marred by juvenile delinquency. A few weeks ago I knocked on a door and a little junior high kid came to the door. He invited me in and very graciously offered me a seat on a rickety divan. The moment his mother came out, she took one look at the boy and started working him over. She gave him a severe tongue lashing for something he hadn't done and shouted, "Get out of here," and he took off.

We proceeded to discuss the problem at hand. "You know," she said, "the trouble with that boy is that he can't do anything right."

I said, "Ma'am, I hate to disagree with you, but you're wrong—dead wrong. Your boy gave me the most gracious invitation into your home I've received in a long time. He invited me to have a seat and made me at home. I'm proud of your boy. And, lady, unless you start to get proud of him, you may never have anything of which to be proud."

Are you backing your youth or are you nailing them to the wall? The average teenager in America doesn't need any critics; he's got critics a dime a dozen. He needs somebody to support him. And the same thing is true of the little tyke.

Do you communicate your love? Do you know how to? By spending time with him. By imparting something of the most precious possession to him in all the world. That's *you*.

I was committed to attend a conference and speak at a banquet. The banquet came on Friday night; I had to fly out early Saturday morning. And there was dictating to finish up at the office. I got all this done, tore home in my car and, just as I turned into the driveway, the lights fell on my boy's bicycle tire.

Flat! I had promised him I'd fix it—just like you have—tomorrow. "Sorry, I just can't get to it, Bob; next week . . . next weekend," you know, on and on. Finally I looked at that tire and realized, boy! this was it! So I fixed it, tore off across town to the banquet and got there late.

"Where in the world have you been?" asked the relieved emcee.

"I'm awful sorry," I said, "but I had a flat."

"I thought you had a new car," he said.

I said, "I do. My boy's bicycle tire." So I firmly, I trust graciously, told him there were times when it was far more important for me to fix my boy's bicycle tire than to eat a banquet meal.

Later, my pal and I were tossing stones into a little creek that runs through a nearby park. I turned to him and said, "Hey, Bob, do you love me?"

"Sure do, Dad, sure do. Man, yeah!"

I said, "Swell, buddy. Why?"

"Oh, shucks! I don't know."

"Now look, pal," I said, "you never want to do or say anything without a reason."

So he sat there tossing things into the creek, and, frankly, I forgot about it. All of a sudden, "Hey! Dad, I've got a reason."

I asked, "Why?"

" 'Cause you fixed my bicycle tire and because you have time to play ball with me."

A third essential is a positive, constructive home life. Ask yourself, "Is my home a magnet or is it a refueling stop?"

People keep asking me, "What in the world do you do about television?" The reason the average kid looks so long at TV shows is that he has nothing else to do. He needs a more constructive home life. "What do you do for recreation?" you ask. "Where do you get ideas? What do you do?"

You don't have to go out and pay thirty bucks to have a good evening. One of the greatest needs in home life today is for more creative thinking—to really get down to some good, wholesome times of fun. Laughter unites. Do you laugh very much in your home?

Let me ask you a question I have pondered myself in the last few months. Do your children understand your Christianity primarily by what you do *not* do or by what you *do*? Many Christians are only distinguished by what they don't do. They don't do this. They don't do that.

There are things we shouldn't do. But the hallmark of Christianity is the reality of a life. And the children know. They know whether I've got the genuine commodity or not because I live with them. I can't pose a front 24 hours a day. Reality is bound to crop out. This is primarily what you communicate to your child: not what you say but what you are.

Allow your child the luxury of a mistake. To let him make his own choice and, when he does, abide by it without ridicule is extremely difficult. Little by little, give your children choices, decisions to make. As they grow older give them more responsibility. Then, finally, when they move out from your home, they can make their own decisions.

We must surround our children with a fortress of prayer. This involves far more than praying in family worship and at meals. Paul said, "Pray without ceasing," or uninterruptedly. This involves a spirit of prayer in a home in which a child grows up realizing there is one person paramount in his home: the living God.

Your child knows if you are totally dependent on God by what happens in your home. It is often in the most informal situations in the home or on the football field that opportunities open up to teach him your complete dependence upon Almighty God in prayer.

Over my years of work with young people I have come to realize there are many praying parents of teenagers in trouble. And it is never too late to pray. But, tragically, our kids often have to get messed up before we recognize our failure in prayer.

Finally, trust the Spirit of God to do for your children what He alone can do.

We can trust Him for our eternal salvation, but we don't trust

Him for the next 24 hours with our children. We're so afraid He just can't handle them. God *will* enable you to do what He has commanded you to do.

I love the epitaph God wrote for Abraham in Genesis, chapter 18. He said, "For I know him, that he will command his children and that they shall keep the way of the Lord." ●

Family Fun Can Be Done

by Mel Larson

Our family had a great time last night! We didn't spend any money, either. In fact, we didn't even leave the house. Our son Jim, 10, showed us how to put a hard-boiled egg through the neck of a milk bottle. Then he took it out again—without breaking it. What was so great about this? Well, because it brought us a fresh sense of family unity.

Today's family is not as closely knit as it was even a decade ago. Why? One reason: families aren't having fun together anymore. Seldom do you see the whole household pitching in on a family project, or singing favorites around the piano, or organizing their home-grown instrumental ensemble.

You can blame TV, the second car, changing mores, Mom's and Dad's breakneck pace. A board meeting on Monday night takes Dad away and another event on Wednesday grabs Mom. The ball game and social on Friday night snags Johnny and Sue. Before long the family unit is riddled and family fun crowded out.

Are any families doing something about this? We asked three about the problem, and to our pleasant surprise we found they were. All three were Christian families, so fun as such was not their immediate goal in life. Yet the parents realized they needed to spend more time together as a family. With special effort to work family recreation into their busy schedules, they had at least partly solved the problem. Here is what I learned.

Family A: This family has a son who just hit junior high. It has had a policy for many years now of designating each Friday night as "family fun night." They rotate, with the son saying what they do one Friday night, the mother next, father next, then back to the son. The person whose "night it is" decides what the family is to do that night. The others go along.

Family B: Mom, Dad, four sons. Sunday evening before church, without fail, is popcorn time. Tuesday and Thursday are potential fun nights, but Dad is away from home often on these nights. They play a variety of games, many of them in the "think" bracket. Summer is picnic time, with a goal of one a week. The backyard is geared for badminton.

Family C: Four in the family, a girl and boy plus Mom and Dad. I talked to the girl first. Her favorite is spin the bottle. Popcorn night was next, plus going on picnics (she liked hikes with Dad while Mom takes a nap).

The boy listed a local hamburger spot first, then long trips, checkers, Mom or Dad reading to him.

So if you want to have fun in your family, you can do it. But it will take some rearranging.

Let me give some suggestions. What works for one family, may not work for another, but try these tips and see what happens.

- Consider the age level of the children. This will largely determine what you do for fun. When babies are small the extra work often keeps fun to a minimum.
- Make a list of the recreational areas in your region. Have you noticed how often visitors or vacationers discover something nearby you have missed for years? And don't forget any nearby state parks. They are ideal sites to take your family camping.
- Find out what the members of your family like to do. As a parent you may have been barking up the wrong tree for a long time—insisting the children like what you like.
- Be definite in your planning. If you can pinpoint a fun period, it will build up anticipation from week to week. Dad's work schedule often is the key element here, along with the activities in church, school and other places.
- Be willing to spend a little money on good equipment and games. But be wise in what you buy. See that it fits age and interests. It's better to buy a bigger bat than a smaller one which Billy will outgrow in a few short months.
- Rediscover what you have within the four walls of your home. With all the toys on today's market, the most enjoyable fun usually comes from the simple.
- Include games which have a spiritual side to them. Your Christian bookstore can help you here.

God's basic unit in society is the family. He knows the stresses and strains in the family and He also knows how we need to relax and have fun. It could be that more fun in your family could be one of God's ways to solve some of the spiritual problems as well, for a family that is tense with each other is bound to have its problems.

The real danger comes if they begin to associate their problems with Christianity. Or they note that Daddy never has time to play ball because he's always away "doing something for the church." But when your family is having fun together, the neighborhood gets to know about it. And in God's provision you may find the door open to share with some of those neighbors the real foundation for your family well-being—the Lord Jesus Christ. ●

Why Christian Homes Fail by Lars I. Granberg

Does your Christian faith affect your family life?

"Ah!" you say, "it does affect it. I attend church regularly, go to midweek service, tithe my income, sing in the choir, teach Sunday school, and avoid worldly forms of amusement."

But if that is the limit to which it is affected, you have a false understanding of the Christian life. This is one reason why we so often have the wrong kind of family life. And this is one reason why Christian homes often fail.

Do not misunderstand. Of course it is important to attend worship faithfully, exercise responsible Christian stewardship, and contribute one's talents and energies. But to regard these as the hallmarks of Christian living is to fall into the Galatian error. This is a heresy as old as mankind. It creeps out in one form or another in every generation, but always with the same aim: to let me keep spiritual score on myself and my neighbor, so I can tell God where I stand. This false view of the Christian life substitutes rules for relationships, demands for understanding, and judgment for love. And in so doing it badly misses the point.

The great words of Holy Scripture are love, forgiveness, reconciliation, and fellowship. These constitute the message of the Gospel. They set the tone for how we do what we do, and make clear that it is the spirit in which we relate to God and live with each other that differentiates the spirit of Christ from its pious-appearing counterfeit.

The false view leads to a spirit of judgment. There is much emphasis on appearances, on blame, on avoiding criticism. In a home dominated by such an atmosphere people become defensive. Some pull into a shell. Some stay away from home as much as possible. Others fight back in subtle or obvious ways.

It is just this kind of self-satisfying bitterness and vengefulness that our Lord came to heal. The life-giving force is that special kind of love which helps us work constantly at understanding, forbearing, forgiving, consideration, and courtesy—and not only at such times as we feel the other is deserving. It is a love which places warm fellowship higher than one's own ego. It prompts the Christian to take the initiative to keep things right rather than allowing us the luxury of nursing an injury or insisting that because we feel wronged the other must make it right.

Probably the biggest problem among our staunchest Christian families, however, isn't open strife within the family. Nor is it a matter of family members harboring deep bitterness or resentment toward one another. It is characteristic of these families that the members are loyal to each other, quick to help one another build a barn or a garage, and they stand by one another during times of serious need. In one sense we would have to speak of these as close families. Nevertheless, many members of such families feel lonely and uncertain. They express a real hunger for love and compassion. Listen to one fine young person from just such a home:

"One thing I regret about my home is the fact that love was very rarely openly expressed. I am certain that deep love was felt for the other family members, but somehow it was seldom put into words. I think this has stood in my way as I have tried to enter into deep personal relations."

This young person regards the home in which he grew up as good in most ways. Physical needs were met. There was faithful Christian instruction. Parents were thoroughly dependable. But they were somehow not able to express their love directly.

Many evangelical Christians seem to feel embarrassed about their tender feelings. Sometimes they teach their children that these are personal and not to be worn on the sleeve. There is suspicion that those who openly express love are shallow or false. (On the other hand, they do not quit spending money because some money is counterfeit.) They insist that when children are given plenty of good food, shelter, warm clothing, care when sick, proper training and discipline, and many other needful things, it should be obvious to them that their parents love them.

Alas, it isn't that simple. Actions are open to more than one interpretation. The home situation described can be explained on the basis of duty as well as love. Most children—most people, for that matter—are uncertain enough of their own lovableness to need at least an occasional unmistakable declaration of affection, for they know they often disappoint those they love.

When you think about it, there is a strange inconsistency found in these situations. Parents are distant and hesitant about expressing love, but rarely do they feel the same about expressing disappointment or disapproval. When the child or spouse is deemed to be in need of reproof, there seems to be no hesitancy at all about "wearing one's feelings on his sleeve." Disapproval is expressed clearly in words of one syllable. Why is this? Why is it important to be clear and unmistakable about disappointment and disapproval, while the other person is left to guess about approval and affection?

A usual result of an inconsistent approach such as this is to leave a child quite clear on what is wrong, but rather fuzzy regarding what is right. This creates the kind of morality which is preoccupied with avoiding what is wrong rather than with achieving what is good: the morality of the Pharisees, leading to the Galatian misunderstanding of the Christian life.

A few suggestions: The key to understanding companionship begins with the desire to communicate love, respect, understanding, and forgiveness. Such love recognizes human frailty, hence does not make extra trouble through unrealistic expectations. Neither does it wait for the other to take the first step in healing broken or strained relationships. It is necessary always to bear in mind that it is not easy to convey accurately one's thoughts and feelings to another, for each of us has his own private world through which we interpret what we see and hear. Therefore we need to take pains to make our thoughts, feelings, and intentions as clear as we can. Above all, give the other person the benefit of the doubt—even when there doesn't seem to be any doubt.

This is not easy. No wise person expects it to be. There is risk. People do get hurt. But it is richly rewarding. Through such efforts one learns what the Biblical statement means when it says that a man who wants to save his life must be willing to lose it. Learning to give when we'd rather nurse a grudge, and love when we'd rather be loved moves us toward Christian maturity. And in such a family atmosphere, your Christian home will not fail.

Small wonder that when the Apostle Paul set down the qualifications for leadership in the church, he put great emphasis upon a man's having first learned to shepherd within his own household (1 Tim. 3:4,5). To create a family situation where people feel mutually responsible for shepherding each other is to make Christianity real at home. ●

Fathers – Fit or Flat?

by John Warder

Dad, what are you doing about your family's physical fitness?

As a father, I know that your main concern is working to put food on the table.

And if you're a mother, a good part of your day revolves around meal planning, cooking, and seeing that everyone gets enough of the right foods at the dinner table.

But too many families stop there and equate fitness with fullness. Physical fitness involves more than eating enough food. It involves a threefold formula that many are familiar with, but which too few families practice: eating the right foods, getting proper rest, and *exercising regularly*.

The first two ingredients—food and sleep—fall fairly naturally into one's schedule.

Granted, you may need to learn to push yourself away from the table a little sooner, and click off the TV before the late news. But generally our hunger drive and need for sleep keep these first two fitness ingredients in balance.

"Regular exercise," though, is a requirement that makes us all cringe a little.

We envision tired muscles, labored breathing, and physical exhaustion. Yet with a minimum of effort and creativity you and your family can form your own little exercise club and discover the joy of developing firm, healthy bodies together.

First, it's good to keep in mind at least two good reasons why your family needs to keep physically fit (you might want to post this on your refrigerator or at the top of your physical fitness progress chart).

Number One: from a physical standpoint, we know from research that: the physically fit person is better able to withstand fatigue for

longer periods of time, is better equipped to tolerate physical stress, has a stronger and more efficient heart, and there is a relationship between mental alertness and physical fitness.

Number Two: from a biblical perspective, God has given the father (husband) the full responsibility for the family's discipline, and physical discipline is no small part of one's well-being (Eph. 6:4). It's interesting that physical discipline carries over into our spiritual lives.

Paul recognized the importance of spiritual discipline and "buffeting" his body when he admonished the church of Corinth: "Do you not know that those who run in a race all run, but only one receives the prize? Run in such a way that you may win!" (1 Cor. 9:24).

And because our bodies are temples of the Holy Spirit, we actually glorify God by being fit (2 Cor. 6:17).

Is every member of your family glorifying God in his or her body? Or are there some "tubby" temples among you? If so, now is the time to institute the "winning program" that Paul talks about.

Fortunately, there are several proven, enjoyable programs to help you meet this challenge as a family.

The two suggested below are inexpensive books which you'll find in most bookstores.

The New Aerobics, by Kenneth H. Cooper, M.D., M.P.H., is one which incorporates activities such as walking, running, swimming, and cycling.

The whole aerobics idea is to get your cardio-vascular (heart and circulatory) system "in shape" by acquiring 30 points per week in your chosen activity. Doing the program together as a family takes about 30–45 minutes per day, and each member will enjoy keeping his own progress chart.

The Royal Canadian Air Force Exercise Plans for Physical Fitness meet the exercise needs of a fast-paced family. The program is made up of a series of body movement exercises—push-ups, sit-ups, bending, and stretching. It takes only 12 minutes to work through it, and the whole family can do it together.

A sense of family unity is developed in a method like this as the kids exercise alongside Mom and Dad.

If these basic suggestions have challenged you to consider the physical fitness of you and your family, why not incorporate one of these programs into your schedule right now? With a little perseverance, you and your family will be skimming over new hurdles. ●

Husbands—and Happy Homes

by Lars Granberg

Any dull party perks up at mention of the biblical teaching that wives are to submit to their husbands as their heads. The self-confident, college-trained wife hears these words with complacent amusement. However, any humor in them is lost on the working wife, who wonders how the family would get along without her weekly pay check.

The American husband often seems embarrassed by the idea of headship over his wife. He is likely to pass the idea off as a joke. When a husband does take the idea seriously, the idea is likely to offend him. "My wife and I have a companionable relationship," he remarks heatedly. "We make our decisions by talking things over and coming to agreement."

These democratic sentiments are in keeping with today's outlook in America. Why not, when wives commonly equal, if not surpass, their husbands in education and breadth of experience. Marriage, as a result, is regarded as a partnership in which there is no junior partner. This sounds like Utopia to the work-worn, exploited, dominated wives of other lands.

But all is not well in reality. Various observers of the American social scene wring their hands over the high divorce rate, with all the social instability this brings. Efforts at understanding why so many marriages end in divorce has indicated several contributing factors. One is the effect upon marriage of changing roles for men and women in our society. In 1900 the idea of young women running the hurdles or throwing the discus at a track meet was as unusual as to find them as department store executives, physicians, judges, or English Channel swimmers. Today they are all of these things and more. But the change is not an unmixed blessing. While women were being "emancipated," something was happening to the men.

The number of young men rejected or prematurely discharged on neuropsychiatric grounds during World War II was reported at 2½ million out of the 15 million called up. This was shocking. Who was guilty of sapping our young men of moral vigor and emotional resilience?

Some said: "Momism." This was defined as a predatory form of motherhood which kept sons emotionally immature through dependence, pampering and psychological bullying.

It soon became evident that it was not as simple as this. A new villain was unearthed. Clinical emphasis shifted from the overprotective mother to the "inadequate mother." Just about the time many American mothers almost had become afraid to cuddle their sons, they were faced with another hobgoblin: maternal rejection. The inadequate mother is the woman who cannot spontaneously love her children nor give herself freely to them. Such women may be bereft of warm feeling, or may have turned these in upon themselves, or they may have diverted these feelings to careers or causes.

Maternal overprotection or rejection are not trivial matters. Their destructive potential is inestimable. But psychologists quickly turned to fathers. Then the writers blistered the absentee father, the good provider who tried to bribe his children with material benefits but withheld himself from them. If boys were being over-feminized, it was because their fathers were too busy getting ahead financially or spending too much time in civic or church responsibilities or in hobbies and sports that took them away from home. Their sons needed a change from petticoat rule in school and at home. If fathers would make it a point to spend time with their children, it was claimed, many family problems would be greatly diminished.

More recently Margaret Mead, whose sprightly comments on men, women, and the American family are well known, has expressed deep concern over fathers' excessive involvement in the home! Husbands are being over-domesticated, she says.

As evidence she points to his dutiful immersion in Little League ball games, PTA meetings, piano recitals, and his pride in his prowess as a chef at Saturday night backyard barbecues. A corresponding loss in masculine assertiveness and venturesomeness has been the inevitable result, and these are the qualities which have been instrumental in pushing back the frontiers.

Understandably, many of our most alert and best informed people have taken these trends and counter-trends to heart and attempted to govern themselves accordingly. This points to uneasiness about the proper role of men and women as homemakers.

I believe that the basic principles governing family roles which are set forth in the Scriptures are as sound today as they were when Paul was inspired to write them to the Ephesian church. The key phrases are found in the Scripture portion: "Wives, be subject to your husbands . . . for the husband is the head of the wife . . ." An examination of these phrases should make clearer the pattern of relationship called for by them.

Christian marriage is described in the Bible as an organismic unity, "one flesh." This is a unity of two persons who are equal in dignity and worth before God, and who have wholeheartedly pledged their love, loyalty, fidelity, and responsibility to one another so long as both live. Since, however, this is a complex unity, it is necessary that someone should have the chief responsibility.

God, who is a God of decency and order, has not left a detail as important as this to chance. When He calls the husband the head of the wife, this represents His order of things. He is saying that He has given the chief responsibility for the home and family to husbands. "Headship," therefore, means that with this responsibility goes corresponding authority. What then is the nature of the responsibility that accompanies headship?

Economic responsibility comes first to mind. And well it may. Paul tells Timothy to inform the Christians committed to his care that "If anyone does not provide for his relatives, and especially for his own family, he has disowned the faith and is worse than an unbeliever" (I Tim. 5:8). If anything, however good in itself, causes a father to neglect his economic duty toward his family, his life belies his Christian witness.

As a usual thing, however, it is not difficult to impress American husbands with their economic responsibility. Problems are more likely to arise out of the feeling that this is one's major, if not sole, contribution to his family.

If a man places a premium on his ability to provide well for his family, he may withdraw from active family participation. When wives thus become faced with the major responsibility for child rearing, many become anxious, overcautious, and prone to overprotection. Therefore, she needs her husband's involvement in rearing their children.

Psychologists speak of the formative influence of the emotional tone of a home upon children. "Emotional climate" or "emotional tone" refers to the "feel" a home conveys. Some homes are tense and explosive, others filled with warmth and good humor, still others with bickering and criticism. The variety is legion.

My own counseling experience has led me to feel that the most important ingredient that makes up the emotional climate is the cumulative effect of the husband's moods when he is at home.

At this point husbands may object. "Look," they may say, "I'm a commuter. Workdays I leave early and get home late. Except for dinner, I hardly see the children. I know how I feel affects the family, but where do you get that stuff about my mood's being the biggest factor? My wife's with the children far more. Why me?"

This is a plausible objection, but it underestimates the impact of a man upon his home. While the atmosphere of the home is a product of the combined moods of the entire family, father not only contributes the most, he also has greatest power to change things.

Take the situation where mother plans carefully for a festive evening: good food, special table decorations, everyone dressed up a bit more carefully than usual, and everyone cheerily awaiting Dad's arrival so the party can begin. But alas, he was sharply reprimanded by his supervisor (unjustly, he felt) before he left for home, hit a series of exasperating traffic snarls en route, and feels as festive as the intended victim of a cannibal feast. His greeting is a series of irritated outbursts which shatters the festive expectations. Unless he senses what happened and takes steps to remedy the occasion, the meal may be gulped down in frozen silence.

The reverse is equally possible. Let us picture the kind of day in which everything goes wrong for mother. The washer breaks down during the first load of clothes, with mounds of needed clothing waiting to be washed. A swarm of door-to-door salesmen have interrupted her frantic efforts to make up for time lost in making other arrangements to keep the family in clean clothing. One particularly pesky salesman lingered for almost an hour. To get rid of him she finally bought more than $17 worth of stuff she really didn't want.

All day the children have been as pleasant as a bear with a boil on his nose. To top it off, the cake she baked for dessert fell. She is kneeling by the oven frosting the cake with her tears, and the children are brawling again when Dad bursts merrily through the door. He was notified of a promotion. To celebrate, he stopped to buy some long-wanted toys for the children and flowers for mother. After seeing the children restored to humor and tearing at the packages, Dad turns to Mother to see that she gets an extra warm greeting. He assures her that saddleback cake always has been his favorite kind—and suddenly everyone is enjoying himself hugely.

Such situations are not unusual in many homes. One time Dad is the villain; another the hero. This makes it essential that the Christian father give priority to infusing his home with an atmosphere of warmth, forgiveness, wise discipline, and mutual respect among the members of his family. Good family relationships must be considered as of more importance than his pride or his prerogatives, so that he will take whatever initiative is necessary to keep the channels of communication open in his family.

Of course, it is impossible for the husband alone to create a good emotional climate in his home. This comes from the cooperative effort of every member of the family. But his dominant moods and his approach to the other members is the seed pearl.

A warm, friendly emotional climate provides a good foundation for discipline; it provides encouragement, help, and healing as family members seek respite at home from life's buffetings. Possibly its most far-reaching contribution is its aid to the spiritual effectiveness of the home.

The emotional climate either helps or hinders the husband's efforts to discharge his most far-reaching responsibilities—the *spiritual* growth of his family. Any thoughtful husband is bound to feel his inadequacy as he considers the scope of all these responsibilities to his home. But God has invited those who feel their lack of wisdom to ask of Him, "who gives to all men generously and without reproaching" (James 1:5). ●

Families Are for Loving

by Gladys Hunt

One father says he gets nowhere with his family in trying to have "family devotions." The hassle is so frustrating he has given up the whole idea as a failure.

Another father warmly recalls that he was distracted the other evening with many things on his mind. He started to leave the dinner table without having the usual Bible reading and prayer time with his family.

"Dad, come back," one of the children called. "We haven't read and prayed together yet." And the other children chorused, "Come back."

Two fathers in two different families trying to do the right thing. One succeeds and the other stumbles.

What possible variables might account for the difference? What elements may be present in one family that are not in the other?

The family is God's creation to provide a safe place for all of us. We dare not abandon it to secular forces. Instead, we declare its basic importance in the formation of children, in the maturing of all its members, and in the total enrichment of life. Building family unity is vital for your church and community. We need to plan, to dream, to create—not give up in despair.

Every family is made up of diverse personalities, has its own dynamics in interpersonal relationships, and has stresses which are peculiarly its own. Who could possibly be an expert, given all these variables?

Building family unity is a mind-set, an ability to relate to others and to create a climate in which others are free to relate to group members; it is living together, loving together, and being whole people together.

Drastic changes in influence-patterns have occurred in our cultural

history. Traditionally the influence flowed from the grandfather to the father to the son. The grandfather did not expect his son's values to be very much different from his own, although neither the grandfather nor the father necessarily verbalized these values. Rural life meant family members worked closely together. A boy knew his grandfather; they worked together. A girl sat and shelled peas with her grandmother. Immigrant or ethnic groups who maintain close family ties long after arriving in America may still demonstrate this influence pattern. It is the influence of the extended family, not the world outside.

With industrialization came the move to the city. Work took Father away from his home. The consolidated school brought young people into new peer pressure. Peer opinion began to matter more than the values of the grandfather or father, causing a conflict within the child.

Today's child is bombarded with thousands of voices, all with their own confusing messages about values. Communication experts say that the average person sees countless advertisements a day—not always consciously perceived, but passing the eye on the way to school, on the pages turned in magazines and newspapers, on the television and almost everywhere else.

Today's families are subject to this kind of pressure. We need to ask ourselves, "Are Christian parents living as though we were still in the bygone culture?" Building family unity is our daily business. It takes our best thinking, our earnest prayers. It calls us to be God's men and women; to live as models who influence by what we are and what we do and what we say. *We* must be the influencers!

Ever pray for patience, only to find that you didn't have any, as life poured out frustrations on your head?

Maybe you've had that same experience in your concern about building family unity. You've been praying about your leadership, studying and weighing new ideas. Unity has never seemed so important for your family, and suddenly it all fell apart. Your spouse misunderstood you, the children quarreled, and even the dog seemed gruff. You're almost inclined to think your family doesn't know what unity is about, and why not call it quits right now!

Don't be too surprised if this is your experience. Building family unity is important, necessary, and possible in our kind of society.

The problem is that we've had so little help in knowing how to do it as Christians. Many of us have been duped into thinking that the simplest kind of influence pattern would do it: make sure the children have straightened teeth, the right lessons, drink their orange juice, and go to Sunday School!

Instead, we're finding we need to plot, to set a course, to conspire (in the best sense of that word) and become more what God wants us to be if we will make family unity a reality.

As Edith Schaeffer, wife of the founder of L'Abri Fellowship, wrote, "What is a family? A formation center for human relationships—worth fighting for, worth calling a career, worth the dignity of hard work."

Obviously, simply deciding to have a united family does not mean you will experience family unity (although *desire* is the first step in improvement). You can line your family up in a row, bark out orders, force them into your mold, and insist on togetherness by coercion. It may even produce unity for a short time. Meanwhile you have children who are "sitting" on the outside, but "standing and shouting" on the inside.

Families are not composed of things; they are made up of people. They are dynamic, not static. We cannot treat people—whether old or young, large or small—as pieces in the machine of life which we will manipulate. They are made in the image of God. The interplay between family members will be different in each family. Each is his own person. No slick formula will work.

But principles come out of our knowledge of how God treats us. He treats us as individuals; he honors our personhood; he listens; he understands; he loves; he calls us to himself; he shares his life with us. We will need his grace in applying these principles in the lives of our family members. We will need the quickening of his Spirit to flood our minds with fresh ideas and to keep our relationships open and clean.

Our trust is in the living God, who will enliven our family relationships, and he does this as he enlivens us personally. Our hope in building family unity is in God himself.

In a world of conflicting ideas, family members need to hear, "This is truth and this is how we know what is right." We need to know what our values are and why we have them. "Our family does it this way," helps make sense in a maze of ideas.

Security is always more than physical; it is emotional and intellectual. It indicates that there are "fences" so that we know where the boundaries are and feel safe.

Since communication is critical to family unity, to what extent should Christian parents sacrifice to provide time for the family to be together?

Should a father or mother refuse a career promotion if it will mean less time at home?

Should a family opt for a simpler lifestyle or lower standard of living to provide for their larger needs of family unity?

Should parents limit participation in church activities or school activities to allow for family togetherness?

These are important questions to consider and act upon.

For the good of the whole, some members must surrender their first preferences. Whatever the activity, it is important because people are so important, not because the activity itself is so important. If the adventure causes stress (whether grumbling or genuine hardship) remember you are building something more than the moment. The experience can be your best opportunity to highlight what is valuable.

Ephesians 4:32 says, "Be kind to one another, tenderhearted, forgiving one another, as God in Christ forgave you."

God's great plan is to redeem us by loving us. In his lovingkindness to us, he gave a pattern for family life that enables us to mirror the gospel in family relationships.

We can accept one another, as God in Christ accepted us.

We can be kind, tenderhearted, knowing none of us is perfect.

We can forgive one another because Christ has forgiven us.

Kind, tenderhearted, forgiving to each other—every day. The Bible is full of wisdom for building family unity, but those three words are the heart of unity. ●

I Didn't Know Dad Loved Me

by Ney Bailey

I remember when I was six years old. I was barely three feet tall, standing on the edge of the municipal pool. "Jump, Ney Ann!" coaxed my father, his arms outstretched. "I'll catch you!"

The water was over my head where he was standing in the pool. I was petrified to jump in.

I called out, trembling, "No, I can't do it!"

"Yes, you can," he shouted. "Jump, and I'll catch you!"

Finally I jumped. But my father wasn't there. My head went under the water, and I came up sputtering and thrashing. Daddy had moved back in the water, hoping I would swim to him. I began to cry.

"Daddy, you moved! You said you wouldn't!"

I heard him laughing. "Ney Ann, you've gotten upset over nothing. You know I wouldn't let anything happen to you. I was just trying to teach you to swim."

That experience had a devastating effect on my childlike mind. I had trusted Daddy with everything that my little heart could muster—Daddy had said he would catch me, but he didn't. He had let me down.

The experience was representative of how I began to feel about him as I grew older. I began to realize that some of the deepest hurts we'll ever know come from those we care most about, hurts which often result in bruised relationships within our families. And those relationships are often the hardest to heal. With many other experiences to fuel my feelings and attitudes, my bitterness toward my father was deeply rooted—and full-grown—by the time I entered college.

It wasn't until after I left Arizona and moved to California to begin Campus Crusade's personnel department that I came to a turning point I wasn't even aware I needed.

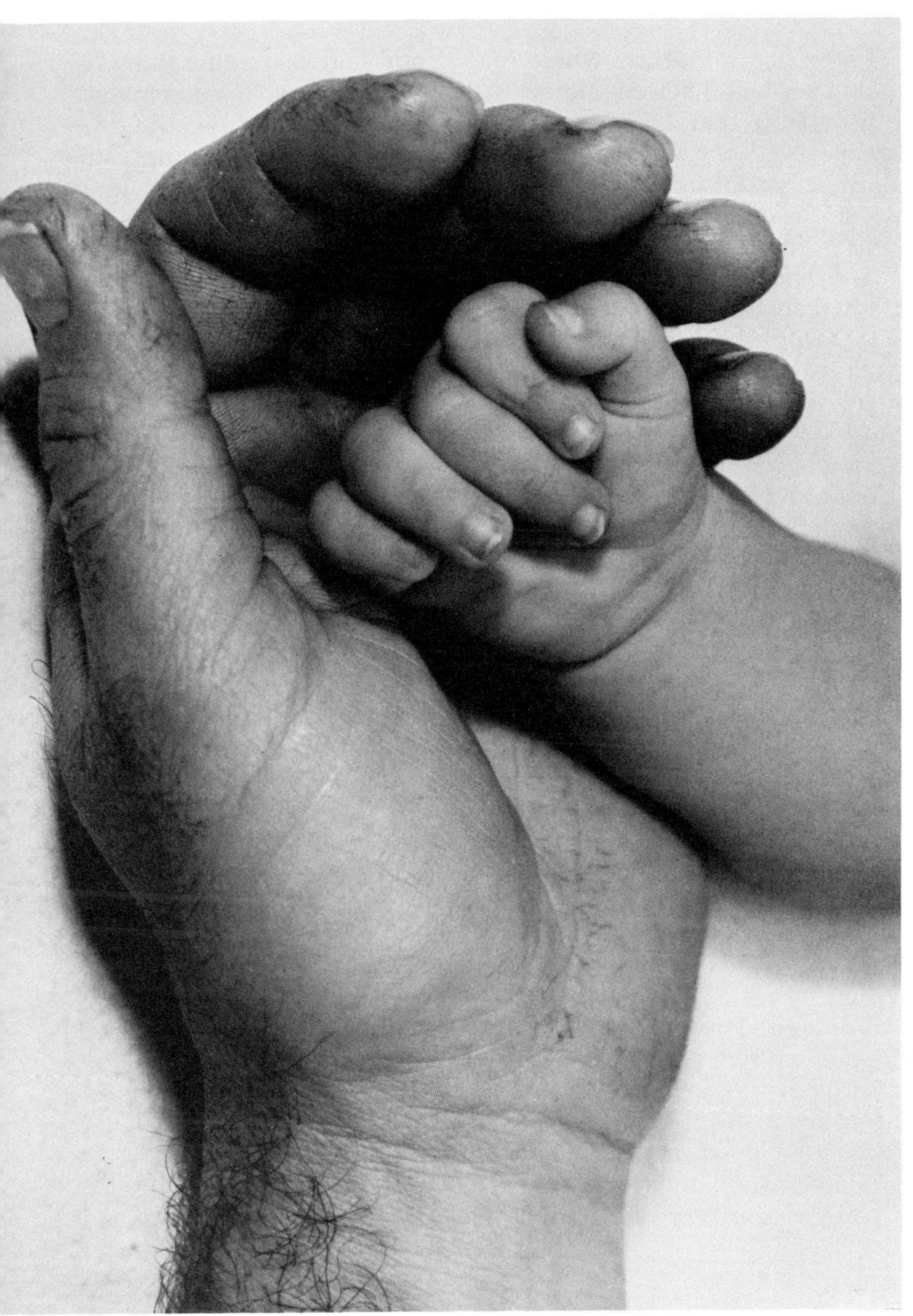

I attended a meeting where one of our staff said some things I had never heard before. I knew that the Bible states, "God is love." I also knew that 1 Corinthians 13 reveals what love is. But the speaker said one thing that was like bright sunshine piercing into a long-closed dungeon: "If God is love, and 1 Corinthians 13 tells what love is, then God loves you and God loves me with that same kind of love."

This was totally new to me.

I had always heard that I was supposed to love other people with a 1 Corinthians-13-kind-of-love. It had even been suggested that I test my own love for others by putting my name in where the chapter mentions "love." I failed the test! But it hadn't occurred to me to put God's name in the place of "love."

Now, I was discovering that God's love toward me is kind, patient, is not provoked, does not take into account a wrong suffered, would bear all things, believe all things, hope all things, endure all things. God's love toward me would never fail.

It was overwhelming to think he loved me in that way.

As I drove home from the meeting, I began to think of my father. I thought of how we had been at odds with each other most of my growing-up years. I knew it was not unusual for a teenager to have conflict with his parents. That was normal enough. But my conflict with my dad seemed much more critical than the norm.

I thought back to the earliest years of my life, when my father had been a struggling law student. Those were the post-depression years, and he studied long and hard, as well as working to help make ends meet. He had very little time to spend with me, and by the time I entered the first grade I hardly knew him. As a result, the major influence in my life was my mother, whom I adored.

As the years flew by and I grew older, I became afraid of my dad. When he raised his voice at my mother or me, something in me shuddered. This fear turned to hostility in my teenage years. My friends' fathers seemed to care about the things they did and the awards they received, but my own father, I thought, was so caught up in his own interests that he didn't care what happened to me. I knew he loved his work, but I felt insignificant to him.

In later years my hostility turned to a subtle rebellion. I thought, "You go your way, and I'll go mine. You don't bother me, and I won't bother you." If Dad yelled at me, I wished I could yell back. If he ignored me, I ignored him. If he hurt my feelings, I'd try to hurt his. I wanted to give him what I thought he deserved.

I thought of how little communication we had and how he seemed to be able only to express his love for me by giving me material things. I didn't feel his love and wondered if it really existed.

I was waiting all those years for him to love me in the way that I wanted to be loved. He never did, so my hate and resentment grew.

Then I heard that message on God's love. I thought, "If God loves my father just the way he is, who am I not to love him also?" My love had been conditional, based on his performance. I had been waiting for him to change. Then, if he changed, I would begin to love him.

Tears began streaming down my face as I drove up the mountain road to my home. For the first time in my life I decided to accept my father just as he was. As I reflected on his background and childhood, I was able to see that he had only given to me out of what had been given to him.

Dad was an only child, raised in a small town north of Shreveport, Louisiana. His parents began having marital difficulty early in his life and soon separated and divorced. He stayed with his mother. She died when he was 13 years old, a great loss to a little boy.

Dad went to live with an aunt and uncle. In the meantime, his father was away most of the time dabbling in oil and investments, making and losing tens of thousands of dollars. He rarely expressed love for his son verbally or emotionally, but he did so materially—demonstrating his care by buying his son gifts and taking him on occasional trips. I could see this pattern repeated years later in the way my father related to his own family.

On the other hand, my mother was the youngest of four daughters, raised on a wheat farm in the small community of Jet, near the Oklahoma panhandle, where her parents had pioneered the land. Her family was characterized by love and closeness, sharing together such activities as daily farm chores, recreation, harvesting, and attending church.

My mother's family was emotionally and verbally expressive of their appreciation for one another, demonstrating love through many acts of kindness, and hugs and kisses. And this pattern carried through to Mother's raising of her own family. She kept detailed diaries of my first three years of life, up until my twin brother and sister were born—what I did, words I spoke, what I ate, and how much I weighed. She was always available to take me anywhere I needed to go, and always ready with words of encouragement for my achievements, however small.

As a child, I had computed these many differences between my parents as meaning, "Mother loves me and Daddy doesn't." But now I could see that they both loved me as best they knew how, in light of their particular backgrounds.

I was grateful for this new understanding as I pulled the car into the driveway. It seemed as if the Lord had done something new in my life. I remember one day in particular. We were sitting in the living room together. I was on the couch, and Daddy was in his reclining chair in front of the TV. Soon he fell asleep. I looked over at him in his chair for a long time and then said in a soft whisper, "Daddy, I love you and I accept you just like you are . . . sitting there in your chair."

Over the next days, a strange thing began to happen. As he felt my acceptance, he began to respond with warmth toward me. He seemed to be more caring and sensitive to little things he could do for me. For example, he went to the doctor's office with me when I had to have minor surgery. He waited for me and bought the prescribed medicine at the nearby pharmacy. There was a dress shop near his law office. He brought home three dresses on approval for me to choose which ones I would like to keep.

God was beginning to restore our relationship!

After a visit home many get-togethers later, I gathered my things to leave. At the door, Daddy asked, "When will you be home next?" He had never asked me that before.

"Oh, about the 21st or 22nd."

Smiling, he said, "I'll see you on the 21st."

A couple of days later I talked to my mother on the phone. "Did Daddy say anything to you about our visit?" I asked.

"Yes, he said, 'Ney must be losing her mind! She asked me for some advice.' "

I am convinced that God wants to heal broken or strained relationships—ones filled with tension and lacking in love. Though my father has never asked me to forgive him of anything, the Lord asked that of me. Today I love and appreciate my dad with all my heart.

And now that the hostility in my own heart has been dealt with, I am better able to see his many wonderful qualities to which I had previously been blind. I'm very proud of him. I was thinking recently that, in many ways, my father hasn't changed. But I have. And that's made all the difference. ●

Teach Your Child to Pray by Elva Anson

One night at a meeting of young Christian parents, I asked, "How do you teach your children to pray?" An uncomfortable silence followed my question. Finally a few people shared some of their experiences. Later one father told me, "If the others are like me, they are reluctant to talk about teaching prayer in the family because they don't feel they do a good job. I used to pray with my sons every night, but I quit. At first they missed our times together, but they finally stopped asking for them."

Teaching children to pray should be as natural and easy as teaching them to talk. Yet many people find it very difficult. When children learn to talk, they simply imitate the sounds they hear us make. When they learn to pray, the same principle applies.

Prayer should be woven through life like threads in a tapestry. Praying is our open line to God—a part of spiritual breathing. That's what Paul means when he tells us, "Pray without ceasing" (1 Thess. 5:17). Such communication comes out of a relationship with a God "who never leaves us nor forsakes us."

Although most children seem to have an inborn sense of God, they do not always understand our "spiritual" words. When I told my two-year-old daughter that Jesus is everywhere, she asked in surprise, "Did he get out of my book?"

When Jay's mother told him that Jesus lives inside of us, he worried about how he was going to get out. Janel's mother told Janel the same thing. The next time her mother handed her a glass of water, she said, "But Mama! Won't Jesus get wet?" One day when we came home from church, I heard my daughter tell our neighbor, "We went to God's house today, but he wasn't home."

Our understanding of God may be so intangible that we have difficulty explaining him in terms simple enough for children to understand. We must not put God in a distant heaven, but help our children understand he is always very close to us even though we can't see him.

Teaching children to pray is tied in with learning who they are, what the meaning of life is, and what wholeness means. When you tuck your baby into bed at night, you can tell him, "Daddy/Mommy loves you, and so does Jesus." As he learns to talk, you can pray with him at night. Your prayer should conform to what he understands.

"God, it has been so good playing with Jimmy today. We had such fun playing with his cars. Watch over him while he sleeps tonight. Amen." Then give him a chance to say a prayer, too.

Keep these prayers short and confine them to areas of the child's experiences. If Sue hurt her toe, you might pray, "Lord, Sue hurt her toe today. Please help it to get better and help other people who have pain tonight not to feel alone." Sue's prayer may reflect your concern for other people.

After Carla heard me say,"God, forgive me for not paying attention to Carla when she tried to tell me why she got in a fight with Eric," she quite naturally prayed, "Please forgive me for talking crossly to Mama today."

Prayer has no special language or form. Rather it is spontaneous, natural, honest communication with God. It is the kind of language children use without pretension.

When Janee was two, I told her one day that I would put her down for her nap as soon as I finished the dishes. I was startled when I hear her in the living room saying very earnestly, "I don't want to go to bed, Jesus." This kind of honesty often disappears from adult prayers.

Sharing with God the intensity of our feelings can be a tremendous relief. One mother who feels strongly about this says, "When my children were very small, I prayed with them. Later I encouraged them to pray alone. I told them that it is important for them to be very honest with God, and there could be things they would want to tell him that they couldn't even tell me."

Just as there are no prescribed words to say and no proper way to speak, there are no proper positions in which to pray. The Bible speaks of kneeling (Luke 22:41), standing (John 11:41), lifting hands

(1 Tim. 2:8), being on a bed (Ps. 4:4). We can pray wherever we are (Ps. 34:15).

A friend of mine who was born in Germany during World War II was raised by her grandparents for the first five years of her life. One of her sweetest memories is of being tucked into bed by her grandmother at night. It was cold in the room, but she was comfortable and cozy as her grandmother listened to her say her prayers. God, to her, is associated with the warmth, security, and comfort she felt while saying her prayers every night.

Many families find that mealtime provides an excellent opportunity for turning their thoughts toward God. In some families each person says a sentence prayer. In others, each one takes a turn thanking God for the day and the food. In my own family, if anyone is missing from the table my husband Everett asks a special blessing on that person. I'm sure it's a comfort for children to know they will be missed and prayed for at the family table.

Staying involved in each other's lives provides support. When I am speaking at a luncheon or other group meeting, I know that my family is praying for me. When my children face a test or fear some involvement with people, they know the rest of the family is praying for them. Paul Jongeward, a busy psychologist, includes his family's plans on his own schedule. He can see at a glance what each member of his family is doing at any hour of the day. He stays actively involved in their lives, praying for specific activities as they come up.

Sometimes in our family we draw names for prayer pals for the week. We don't tell whose name we drew until the end of the week. Other times we look for things in each other to give praise for. At least once a year we set aside a week to celebrate each member of the family. While a person is being celebrated, the rest of the family prays especially for him/her.

Prayer should come out of natural experiences. When we go camping, we often look for an open spot to take a blanket at night to view the stars. The five of us lie on our backs, squashed together for warmth, and gaze at the brilliance stretched over our heads. In the mountains the sky, ablaze with stars, seems so close and awesome. We talk about the wonder of a God who could make such splendor, who knows the number of those stars, and still knows and cares about us. Then we all lie quietly, each talking to God silently as we feel his greatness envelop us.

Occasionally we take our children for a walk and picnic in the woods. As we sit on a fallen log looking at the rustic beauty surrounding us, we sing the song "How Great Thou Art." Especially meaningful is the verse from that song which speaks of the woods and forest glades, the birds singing in the trees, the mountain's grandeur, the brook, and the breeze.

Songs such as "The Birds Upon the Treetops," "Jesus Loves Me," "Let the Beauty of Jesus Be Seen in Me," and many more are excellent ways to teach children to pray. Young children love to make up their own songs or poems to express their joy and praise. Encourage this creativity. Let them draw pictures that describe their prayers of gratitude, or even write "love letters" to God.

God intends for children to learn from their parents what it means to be unconditionally accepted, to be loved, and to have their specialness appreciated and encouraged. He wants parents to live in forgiveness and demonstrate the joy of living Christianity.

"Forgiveness," says one youngster, "is when you spill a carton of milk all over the kitchen floor, and your mom says 'accidents will happen'."

God tells us that if we, who are earthly, give good gifts to our children, how much more our heavenly Father will take care of his children. If we can forgive our children, how much more God will forgive us.

When we have introduced our children to God, who is our best friend as well as our Father, we can come with our children to sit at Jesus' feet and learn together how to reach out to him. ●

Bringing Down the Parent-Teen Wall

by Roy B. Zuck

"My folks are so old-fashioned they creak! Here I am 14, and they won't even let me have my first date! And besides, they criticize every move I make at home. According to them, I never do *anything* right. Why don't they let me grow up?"

"I just can't understand the teenagers in our home. They don't seem interested in us parents anymore. They turn a deaf ear to our demands. Our teens seem to think they should have everything they want and be able to go any place they like. Difference of opinions over the use of the car, TV, and telephone frequently cause sparks of contention in our home. According to our youngsters, we are nothing but tyrants."

These plaints—by teens and parents, respectively—indicate that living in the same house with people between the ages of 12 and 18 is not always easy.

Nine million American homes have teenagers in them. And that often means about as many problems! Sadly enough, even *Christian* homes are often miserable places in which to live. Christian young people have confided in their pastors and teachers that home is often the *last* place they'd rather be. "After all," they say, "who wants to hang around when parents are nagging at us and don't understand us?"

Deep inside, most, if not all, Christian parents honestly want to help their young people to understand and be close to them, to be able to guide them in godly paths. But with a concerned, shoulder-shrugging attitude, Christian parents plead, "What can we do? How can we make our home life enjoyable, not just bearable?"

Also, many teens honestly want to get along better at home. According to a survey of 2,000 young people in a leading denomination, the modern Christian teenager "feels a twinge of conscience that he's not as considerate of his family as he ought to be, wishes he could understand his parents better, and finds it difficult to confide in them." The same survey revealed that Christian youth are disturbed by the fact that their family members aren't "close" and don't talk over their problems together.

Parents and teens want to understand each other, but the family communication lines are often down.

Why? There are at least three reasons.

First, teens are no longer children. Young people want to be independent and be treated as adults. But this is the problem! They desire independence, but also need parental security to fall back on. They need understanding parents to depend on. Therefore you need to know how much "rope" to give them, how much free rein to allow them. Parents who fail to understand this independence-dependence dualism invite home havoc.

Second, young people are often befuddled by conflicting standards. Through the broadening experiences that come with growing up, teens are keenly aware that the world's standards differ greatly from God's biblical standards upheld in Christian homes and churches. As a result young people are susceptible to the satanic trick that says, "Your parents are old fogies. They don't want you to follow the world and have a good time. This shows that they aren't really interested in you."

Wise Christian parents, of course, don't just plunk a list of rules for Christian conduct on top of teens and expect them to follow the orders slavishly. These parents talk over principles of Christian conduct with their young people and seek to help their teens accept those principles as their very own. Discussion on *why* certain things are out of bounds for Christians is as necessary as the simple assertion, "These are wrong."

Third, parents as well as teens are going through a period of adjustment. After all, most parents have never lived with teenagers before! Parents may fear that if they are too lenient, they may be inviting moral disaster for their fledglings. And yet they may be concerned that too many rules will only result in rebellion by their adolescent offspring.

What, then, can be done? How can the parent-teen wall in Christian homes be broken down? Here are some suggestions:

1. *Set the example.* If your young people don't attend church regularly, read the Bible daily, and exercise Christian virtues by the power of the Holy Spirit, is it because *you* don't? In a recent survey by the National Sunday School Association on why teens quit church, a teenager in Minnesota said it was easy to quit going because his folks didn't go. Verna Joiner, in her interesting book, *What Teens Say* (Warner Press), quoted a young person who said, "My father knows the Bible and talks a lot about religion, but he doesn't live it."

1 Timothy 4:12, directed to young people, applies to parents as well: "Be thou an example of the believers, in word, in conversation [conduct], in charity, in spirit, in faith, in purity." If you want your young people to love the Lord and be growing in him, be sure you are too!

2. *Don't withdraw controls.* Teens may resent restrictions now, but in a few years they'll thank you for it. Their growing toward adulthood is no excuse for letting them do as they please. Teens inwardly resent parental irresponsibility toward their conduct.

3. *Be firm, loving, and fair.* Immerse your demands in the atmosphere of genuine love and concern. "Fathers, do not arouse your children's anger" (Eph. 6:4a, Berkeley). A calm but firm manner gains far more respect than loud outbursts of anger. And never publicly condemn a teen for a shortcoming. After all, we all make mistakes.

4. *Bend an understanding ear.* If your adolescent wants to talk with you, don't listen "half-way" while you keep on reading the newspaper. As you listen to his problem, try to see it from his point of view. Try to sense how teens feel in and react to various situations. One girl wrote, "I like my family very well, but I do wish my parents would be a little more understanding."

5. *Talk with your teens.* In conversation, talk *with* your young people, not down, at, or to them. As much as you may hate to admit it, they are no longer your "little children."

6. *Be interested without being nosy.* Show genuine interest in their activities, but respect their privacy. Don't barge into their room without knocking. And never open and read their mail. Remember that young people are *people.* Constantly apply this test to your life: "Are *all* my actions pleasing to Christ?"

7. *Develop "familyship."* Do things together that teens are interested in. This means things like playing Ping Pong, going camping, etc. Let them invite their friends over. Make home a fun center, not just a restaurant-motel combination.

8. *Maintain regular family worship.* Don't commit the error of thinking that family devotions need to be long to be good. Keep them brief, as well as varied and relevant. Let your teens sometimes lead devotions. According to one survey among Christian teens, family devotions is one thing they *want* regularly. Family worship and consistent Christian living help you fortify your teens with the bedrock foundation of biblical truths and Christian standards. "Bring them up in the instruction and admonition of the Lord" (Eph. 6:4a, Berkeley).

9. *Keep on praying and trusting the Lord.* Nothing works like fervent prayer! (James 5:16) And no attitude toward the Lord is so needed as patient trust and confidence (Prov. 3:5). Don't run ahead of or rush the Lord. Give God's Spirit time to work in the hearts of your youth. Pray that in God's own time and way, He will lead them into His will.

10. *Remember that the disease of teenageitis is temporary.* Keep in mind that your offspring won't remain in adolescence forever. Continue exercising the above suggestions, and it may not be long before your young people will rise up and call you blessed (Prov. 31:28). ●

Here's How, Fathers

by John M. Drescher

To become a father biologically requires little commitment or knowledge, but to *be* the father that God intends is one of the most rigorous and rewarding responsibilities of a man's life. It involves the full spectrum of the emotional and spiritual dimensions of existence. To be a Christian father means time, teaching, right priorities, love, and spiritual example.

Paul, in addressing the fathers in the Ephesian church, placed family responsibility squarely upon the shoulders of husbands and fathers. He identifies specific duties. First, as a husband, the man is to "love his wife as Christ loved the church and gave himself for it." This is basic. How can a father fulfill family obligations while he is occupied with making a living, contributing to the community, and sharing in church ministry? By loving his wife!

A statement made famous by Charlie Shedd in his book *Promises to Peter* is true. He says, "The best thing I do for my children is to love their mother well." Shedd may have been the first to say it that way, but Paul said basically the same thing.

When husbands show sacrificial love to their wives, they instill a sense of worth in their children. And when the partnership of husband and wife remains in good repair, the parenting of children will result in loving and right relationships.

Scripture also directs: "And you fathers, provoke not your children to wrath; but bring them up in the nurture and admonition of the Lord" (Eph. 6:4). From beginning to end, Scripture pictures the father as the teacher of his children and the guardian of the family's spiritual riches. A father dare not palm off his responsibilities to his wife, the church, or anyone else. Scoutmasters, school coaches, or movie heroes can never replace Dad. At times they become a fill-in in the mind of a child whose own father fails in taking time for him.

Discipline

The term "nurture" literally means to educate, train, or instruct with the aid of discipline and correction. And the word discipline comes from the word "to learn" or "to disciple." Sometimes discipline is thought of essentially as punishment, but it is much broader than that. It includes the entire process of training and caring for the physical, the mental, the moral, and the spiritual.

Children need to learn that life has structure. No one can ignore the basic principles of life and be a happy, useful person. The pamphlet *What Every Child Needs*, produced by the National Association of Mental Health, Inc., says it clearly: "Every child needs to know that there are limits to what he is permitted to do and that his parents will hold him to these limits."

So there needs to be punishment when wrong is done. This is a part of discipline. But the other important part of discipline is to encourage.

Martin Luther's father was very strict, and his famous son used to say: "Spare the rod and spoil the child—that is true; but beside the rod keep an apple to give him when he has done well." Philosopher-theologian W. Robert Smith, in an article "Why God Gave Children Parents," writes, "Our children go bad because we say only 'Don't! Don't!' and they think all of life is negativism."

Benjamin West tells how he became a painter. One day his mother went out leaving him in charge of his little sister Sally. In his mother's absence he discovered some bottles of colored ink and began to paint Sally's portrait. In doing so he splattered ink over the table and floor. When his mother returned she saw the mess but said nothing. She picked up the piece of paper and looked at his drawing. "Why," she said, "it's Sally!" and she stooped and kissed him. West said, "My mother's kiss that day made me a painter." Encouragement did more than rebuke could do.

It is noteworthy that the New Testament statement about father and child opens with a word of kindness in contrast to statements about the "rod" so frequent in Proverbs. Here Paul says, "Don't provoke your child to wrath." Also in Colossians 3:21 he writes, "Fathers, provoke not your children to anger, lest they be discouraged."

Fathers are more likely than mothers to be carried away with anger and punish the child excessively. This quick and angry punishment as well as a continual spirit of criticism and rebuke can break the spirit of a child. Discipline that is harsh and unfair will not instruct or educate; it will frustrate. So fathers are called to show firmness with gentleness.

Father and mother should see themselves as a team in discipline. Gibson Winter, in his fine book *Love and Conflict,* points out that parents must make basic decisions together. This brings strength and consistency in discipline. It also saves the mother from gaining the image of family enforcer. In the absence of the father, the mother carries out the rules which both have established.

Spiritual Instruction

Scripture directs fathers to bring up their children in the admonition of the Lord. This means to give counsel or training by word, to warn or hold back from the wrong, to reprove for past errors, and to point out dangers in the future. It is summarized in 2 Timothy 3:16—"All Scripture is inspired by God and is useful for teaching the faith and correcting error, for resetting the direction of a man's life, and training him in good living" (Phillips).

To the child, the father is God's representative; this makes the father's task sacred and serious. We fathers are to deal with our children as God deals with us.

Father sets the example of godliness in the family. There are two ways to instruct: one is to teach by imparting facts and knowledge; the other is to teach by example. To "train up a child in the way he should go" refers primarily to example.

When God revealed to Abraham that he was to be the father of a great nation, his duties as a father were outlined. God said, "For I know him, that he will command his children and his household *after* him, and they shall keep the way of the Lord, to do justice and judgment; that the Lord may bring upon Abraham that which he hath spoken to him" (Gen. 18:19).

The power of example and teaching is also linked in Deuteronomy 4:9–10. "Only take heed to thyself and keep thy soul diligently lest thou forget the things which thine eyes have seen, and let them depart from thy heart all the days of thy life; but teach them to thy sons, and to thy son's sons. . . . And I will make them learn to fear me all the days that they shall live upon the earth, and that they may teach their children."

In Deuteronomy 6 the point is again stressed that the Word of God shall first be in the heart of the parent and then it will be effective in the life of the child. Cannon Lumb wrote, "Religious words have value to the child only as experience in the home gives them meaning." So whatever a father wants his child to be, he himself must be that kind of person.

Fatherly Love

Father is responsible for setting the atmosphere for the family. Here the child may learn either that love is the greatest power or that force is. Children vitally understand God's love, mercy, forgiveness, and acceptance through Jesus Christ to the extent they experience these same relationships in the home. The most significant religious experiences of a family consist of the things that go on between family members as they go about ordinary things day by day. A daughter will most likely learn how to judge a man from the pattern she sees in her father. If a father is godly and happy, she will likely pick out that kind of a man for a husband.

A college classmate of mine once wrote me: "My just-turned-four daughter has been praying the Lord's Prayer now for some time. It jars me sometimes to realize that Dawn's first concept of her Father in heaven is based on her concept of and relationship with her father on earth. If her father on earth is consistently too busy to spend time with her, will she easily be able to think of her Father in heaven as the One who assures her, 'Call unto me, and I will answer thee'? If her father on earth demonstrates no compassion for her hurts, will the assurance that 'like as a father pitieth his children, so the Lord pitieth' have any meaning for her? If her father on earth is most concerned about his work and his wealth, will she be able to grasp the tremendous significance of the Good Shepherd laying down his life for the sheep?"

May God help us fathers to enable our children to see the translation of the living God in our lives. High calling; high rewards. ●

Are You Fun to Live With? by Bruce Larson

1-10-85

Lee Whiston dropped a bomb in the middle of our weekly luncheon meeting of Christian businessmen in midtown Manhattan when he asked us, "Are you fun to live with?"

God used that question to check my own motives and attitudes. Why do I want my wife or my children "to be more Christian" at times? Is it because I want God's best for them or because I want God to change some annoying trait in their life that is creating a problem in mine? Is my motive really love—or am I using God to nag my family?

The home is the most difficult—and rewarding—place for any Christian to put his faith to work. It's much easier to be effective and loving and faithful and gentle with people we only see from time to time. Unfortunately, we cannot fool the people who share our home. I am convinced that *we are what we are at home!*

At the heart of our Christian conviction is the belief that God wills newness of life, peace, joy, and love, not only for individuals, but for families. Here are four things that God has been trying to show our family over the years so that we can cooperate with His purpose and plan for us.

If you really want God to make your home new, you must let Him begin with you. It is difficult for the member of the family, whether parent or child, who thinks he is "farthest along spiritually" to make the first move in a total surrender of his will and life to Christ. The instinctive thing is to hope that the others will catch up to us so that we can go "all the way" together. This is never the case. One member of the family must be the spiritual pioneer and become totally vulnerable to the others in the family for Christ's sake to initiate God's action in a home.

Many of us live in a stalemate and cry "Unfair! Unfair!" But the only way to break the stalemate is for one to go all the way. Each going half way is never God's solution for a marriage.

There is an amazing truth in I Peter 3:1 that says, "You wives be submissive to your husbands so that some, though they do not obey the word, may be won without a word by the behavior of the wives." (That verse applies equally to husbands!) How wise Peter was in sensing that we are not to talk about our faith at home, or if we do, to talk very sparingly. The thing that counts is to *live* a new and radiant life day by day and to be "fun to live with."

A second thing that our family must learn again and again is how to love in God's way. We are all aware of how children learn to manipulate their parents. They know how to "butter up" Father for an increase in allowance, the use of the car, or permission to do something forbidden. The tragic thing is that most adults relate to each other in just the same way only with a little more sophistication.

When God's love captures us and we have the resources from within to live out I Corinthians 13, we no longer have to manipulate people, but are free to be vulnerable to them and to their demands. This is what Christ meant in the great commandment to love one another as He has loved us. We have the promise that this kind of love never fails.

My wife and I laugh often at how we must continually learn to give love in terms meaningful to the other. Each of us would rather give love in ways that we enjoy giving rather than in the ways the other enjoys receiving.

When God has convicted her of some failure in our relationship, she has often expressed her love or repentance by baking me a pie. Now I don't especially like pie, but I have had to eat a lot of it in 13 years!

In the same way, I have come home ready to hug and kiss a spouse with whom I was in violent disagreement a few hours earlier. At such a time romance is the last thing that she wants from me!

Well, the thing that we keep learning from God is what to do after He has changed one of our hearts. We need to ask Him *how* to express this new love that we feel so that the other can receive it unmistakably. God wants to love people through us and He has to show us His unique strategy for loving each person He sends us.

I got a great deal of help a few years ago from a small group we belonged to in Illinois. One of the couples was concerned about a preschool daughter, their only child. The father, who was extremely busy in all manner of church, civic, and scouting activities, felt that he was so out of touch with his daughter that he would have to drop some worthwhile activities and spend more time with her. He tried this with no results.

One night he came to the group radiant. We knew that God had shown him a new dimension. He told us that God had revealed to him that it was not more time that his daughter needed, but *all of him* for a brief time each day. He said he had been aware that when he was playing games with her or reading to her or doing things with her that he always had part of his mind on something else, or was carrying on a conversation with his wife, or was watching TV. His daughter never had more than half of him. She reacted to this (as all of us do) and had all the symptoms of being unloved and rejected.

When God showed this man that one of the ways to love is to give another our undivided attention, his daughter was literally transformed and the relationship took on a new dimension. This same thing is true for husbands and wives, brothers and sisters, roommates, etc. I will always be grateful for this lesson and have to learn it over and over again in daily life.

The third lesson our family is learning has to do with total honesty. Real communication between God and man or between man and man requires total honesty. Most of us hide behind our masks and pretend to be people we are not. How hungry our family is to know us as we really are and to be known as they really are.

Our children need to know of our past failures and what we did when we were their age. They also need to know of our present failures and where we need forgiveness today. If in our family prayers we can be honest about ourselves, we do more to introduce our children to God than in all of our prayers for them. As a matter of fact, we must do much more praying with them and far less praying at them. (It is best to pray for them in our own private devotions.) In marriage we need to open our hearts totally to a spouse and to learn to say "I am sorry" or "I was wrong" at the appropriate times.

What happens in family prayers after our children see us lose our tempers, become unfair or unjust earlier in the evening and then kneel with them in prayer and pray for all the missionaries around the world and the minister in the church and Aunt Martha and Uncle Jim? They know this is phony and is not really doing business with God at all. When we can include prayers for our present needs in their presence (of which they are all too aware), they will almost invariably respond to the reality of Christ themselves.

The main thing to remember is never to hesitate being honest about yourself, but always hesitate being honest about another.

Yet there are times for us to be honest about somebody else we love. One Christmas morning I received a handsomely wrapped present from my youngest son, which turned out to be a bottle of deodorant. On the card were these words, "Not because you do. So that you won't!" What tact! I have often wished that when it did seem right to talk to somebody else in the family about his needs, that I could have the gift to say things that way. I believe that God will show us how to say things to others about their needs in those rare times that require it.

The final thing that I personally struggle most with is in letting others in the family minister to me. As a clergyman, I have an idea that I must always be right, the source of all Christian truth. Christ tries to show me that He is in my home independently of me and that some of His greatest truths come not only from my wife, but from my children, often the youngest. God is there and He is working and I must enjoy being on the receiving end as others are used by Christ. I believe that I am becoming free of having to bring Christ to my family. I might add that it is a great deal more fun to discover Him already here in our midst.

However, the battle is not easy. About a year ago I was having a difficult relationship with a wonderful Christian man. He seemed to judge me and criticize me no matter what I did. One day he wrote me a letter. I was furious and brought it home to my wife who was cooking dinner. "How in the world can I answer this?" I grumbled. She made several suggestions that I disposed of because I didn't think she understood the devious nature of this man's spirit.

Finally, she stopped frying hamburgers, turned to me, and said, "Why don't you take the advice you're so free to give all the rest of us?" (I knew then something was coming.)

"What is that?" I asked.

"Why don't you admit to God that you have no love in your heart for this man and ask Him to change you?"

"That's ridiculous!" I snapped and stomped out of the room to read the evening paper until dinner was ready.

That night in saying prayers with my ten-year-old daughter, I no sooner got on my knees than I had to face up to what I knew God had been saying to me through my wife. I asked His forgiveness in my daughter's presence and asked God to change me. My daughter concluded her prayers by saying, "Lord, you know that Father is a difficult man to change, and yet we know You can do it, and I ask You to give him Your love for this man."

Now this is not the role I have chosen for myself. I would rather be the teacher, the prophet, and the authority in my home. But frankly, this does not work, and lately I've been coming to enjoy being a learner with my family at the feet of Jesus Christ.

I have been told that traditionally there are two schools of thought in Germany. The industrial, practical, northern part of Germany has this philosophy: "The situation is serious, but not hopeless." In the southern part of Germany, more romantic and perhaps less practical, the philosophy seems to be: "The situation is hopeless, but not serious."

Apart from Christ's love and presence in us, there is not much hope for us and our families, being the kind of people we are. But when we know that Christ is with us and in us and contending for us, we can then look at the grimmest situation and say, "It's hopeless, but not serious." Jesus Christ is alive and loves us and wants to give us and our families joy and peace and love and newness of life! ●

Sign Up for Parenting! by Landrum R. Bolling

Read 1-10-85

Parenthood is a part-time occupation most of us enter almost totally unprepared, never really master, and in some cases, get worse at as the years go by. Having got my children to that age at which I can reasonably believe I have done them about as much harm as I can, having reflected on some things I did and didn't do, having had opportunity as a teacher and college administrator to observe, rejoice, and weep over the parental handiwork of others, I have some free advice on how to learn to be a parent in this bewildering age.

The chances are that you will never be elected president of the country, write the great American novel, make a million dollars, stop pollution, end racial conflict, or save the world. However valid it may be to work at any of these goals, there is another one of higher priority—to be an effective parent. This, like good French cooking, or a velvet lawn, takes time—a lot of time.

So, accept the fact that being a parent is one of the most important tasks you will ever undertake—and budget your time and energy accordingly.

Most of us are fettered with the notion, though we don't say it, that we don't have the time to be parents. So, find the time, and if something else has to go, let it. Neither self-seeking ambition nor service-to-mankind idealism can absolve us of the responsibilities we take on by having children. But the glory of it all is this: among the richest rewards of life can be the mutually fulfilling relations of parent and child who know and love and spend time with each other.

Think long and hard about the particular parental role you have to play—now. Neither instinct nor memories of your own parents will be a sufficient guide. Parenthood has to be learned. We need to read more, discuss more, think more about what our parenthood requires. We need more deliberate education on the subject as part of our regular schooling—and that schooling ought to involve some kind of guided contact with, service to, and learning about children, how they grow and develop. Since most of us never had a chance to get that kind of education for parenthood, we must find substitutes. But try to learn—by reading, by observation, by honest reflection.

Don't regard them as an extension of yourself. A child is not a parent's third arm, a beauty spot on the cheek, or a boil on the neck. A child is not a parent's toy or private thing. A child is a person bent on growing into its own individuality. You cannot fulfill your ego through your child, though many parents try—usually with painful results for both parent and child. Just as you can't build up your own self-esteem by forcing your dream of what you had hoped to accomplish on your children, neither should you beat yourself over their failures. Of course, you will suffer—and particularly if you know that part of the failure is your fault—but again, every person is going to make his own mistakes, even *your* child—and even you.

Enjoy your children. This means more than going on picnics and playing games, but it means that, too. Most of all, it means accepting them with gladness (as much of the time as possible), and expecting to find in your relationship with them part of your own fulfillment.

Love them and believe in them. This isn't always easy, for two reasons. First, they are at times downright unlovable. Second, we are often so frozen up by our own fears, doubt, and self-hate that we can't love and we can't communicate belief in others. As we can grow up we can come to love more fully—ourselves and others. As we can come to know that God loves us in spite of what we are, that we are loved by another person despite our faults, we can come to love our children as we ought and to communicate to them our belief in them. We love and believe in another person not because he has "earned" it, but because he is a creation of God.

Expect something of your children. One of the common faults of present-day parents is not that they overwork and exploit their children—as repeatedly happened in agricultural families—but that they ask nothing of the children. Today's children grow up with a great sense of worthlessness. They perform no helpful, meaningful role in the family or the society. They are parasites—and know it. And resent it. Denied the daily chores farm children have traditionally had to perform as their contribution to the survival of the family, or any adequate substitute, too many children grow up feeling excessively dependent and defensive.

To gain self-respect, confidence, and an ability to deal with real life, a child needs to be able to contribute to the common life, to know that he is counted on to do something useful. If the family cannot provide that challenge within the push-button city home, the family, the church, and the community ought to see to it that some purposeful challenge to young people is provided in the broader community—and serious expectations are placed upon them.

Be honest with them. They want to know, and have a right to know, what we really think and feel. This means we have to talk out what is in our minds and emotions and why; they aren't mind readers. We can't get away with such easy declarations as "Because I say so," much as we all wish we could. At the same time, when we have explained as honestly and fully as we know how and are convinced we are right, we have to have the courage to stand firm and take the consequences.

Part of being honest is showing our feelings—both joy and sorrow, both weariness and exuberance, both love and hate, both compassion and anger. We cheat our children and ourselves and our relationships when we pretend that we are being calm and sweet and understanding when underneath we are furious. Honest anger is human and inevitable and should be expressed, hopefully within limits and soon to be replaced by reconciliation, but to hide genuine anger is to create smoldering resentment and to promote subtle cruelties—and to rob children of the right to come to terms with real human situations.

Let them go. We do not own our children. In the end we cannot control them, make them over, or save them. In the end, the best we can do for them is free them into the hands of God. The power of truth and love and goodness and beauty works within their souls as much as in our own. They are, ultimately, his children. And he is sufficient to their needs. ●

If I Had Another Chance . . . by John Drescher

Read 1-12-85

"What should I have done differently? If your children were small again, what would you do?"

These words burst from a father sitting across from me. He felt he had failed as a father. Although they came in a blunt way that day, they are not the words of a lone father. In them are questions which are uppermost in the minds of many parents.

What has experience in counseling taught me? Where would I put the emphasis if my children were small again?

Loving

If I were starting my family again, I would love the mother of my children more. That is, I would be freer to let my children see that I love her. It is so easy for parents to assume love, to take each other for granted, and so to let a dullness creep in which can dampen the deepest love.

When a child knows parents love each other, there is a security, stability, and sacredness about life which is gained in no other way. A child who knows parents love each other and who hears them expressing words of love for each other needs little explanation about God's character of love or the beauty of sex.

To let my child know I love his mother, I would seek to be faithful in doing little things for her. True love is visible. I would show special kindnesses such as opening the car door, placing her chair at the table, giving her little gifts on special occasions, and writing her love letters when I'm gone from home. I would take her hand as we stroll in the park. And I would whisper loving words about her in the ears of my children. I would praise her in the presence of my children.

Love is like a plant. It needs nurture. We must do the things love directs or it will shrivel.

Listening

If I were starting my family again, I would do more listening. Most fathers find it hard to listen—we are busy with the burden of work. A child's talk seems like unimportant chatter. Yet we can learn so much more by listening than by talking—especially from our children.

I would listen when my child shares his little hurts and complaints, his joys and what he is excited about. I remember as clearly as the day it happened the time my busy father listened to me as a first-grader when I came home frightened about a situation at school. His calmness and concern, demonstrated in listening to me, relieved my fears. I was ready to return the following day full of courage and confidence. Had he simply said my fear was foolish or had he refused to hear me out, my fears would have grown.

I would seek to keep from staring into space when my child is talking to me. I would try to understand what my child says because I now believe that the father who listens to his child when he is small will find that he will have a child who cares what his father says later in life. I now believe there is a vital relationship between listening to a child's concerns when he is small and the extent to which the child will share concerns with his father when he is in his teens.

If my child were small again, I would stop reading the newspaper when he wants to talk with me. And I would try to refrain from words of impatience at the interruption. Such times can be the best times to show love and kindness.

One evening a small boy tried to show his father a scratch on his finger. After repeated attempts to gain his father's attention, the father stopped reading and said impatiently, "Well, I can't do anything about it, can I?"

"Yes, Daddy," his small son said. "You could have said, 'Oh.' "

These early years are the years for teaching. And by the time the child reaches 15, parents have done most of their teaching. By 15 the child knows what the parents believe. From now on the parent's primary opportunity is to be available when the child comes for help.

Belonging

If I were starting my family again, I would seek to use as many opportunities as possible to give my child a feeling of belonging. This is essential for a child's security and feeling of worth. And when a child feels he belongs in his family and is of real worth there, it is not a big step also to feel accepted, loved, and of worth to others and in God's sight.

Feelings of belonging are generated by doing things together, by sharing common concerns and trusting each other with responsibilities.

Celebrations of birthdays, when the person rather than the gift is central, create a sense of belonging. A sense of belonging is built into the child when prayers are prayed on his behalf, when his opinions are valued, and when he is included in the serious and fun experiences of the family.

He feels he belongs when he is invited to be involved in the responsibility and work of the family. No part of child guidance is more important than assuring the child by action and word that he is important for the family and he has a place in the affections of the family.

Praising

If I were starting my family again, I would seek to be freer to express words of appreciation and praise. Children are reprimanded for making mistakes. But many children seldom hear words of commendation and encouragement when they do a job well or exhibit good behavior.

Will Sessions, discussing the topic "If I had a teenager," says, "I would bestow praise. If the youngster blew a horn, I would try to find at least one note that sounded good to my ear, and I would say a sincere good word about it. If the school theme was to my liking, I would say so, hoping that it would get a good grade when it was turned in. If his choice of shirt or tie, of socks or shoes, or any other thing met my liking, I would be vocal."

Probably no other thing encourages a child to love life, to seek accomplishment, and to gain confidence more than proper, sincere praise—not flattery but honest compliments when he does well.

Playing

If I were starting my family again, I would plan to take time to do more things together. In every father's week there are 168 hours. He probably spends about 40 hours at work. Allow another 15 hours for driving to and from work each week, overtime, and lunch. Set aside 56 hours per week for sleep. That leaves a father 57 hours each week to spend elsewhere. How many are spent with his family?

A group of 300 seventh- and eighth-grade boys kept accurate records of how much time their fathers spent with them over a two-week period. Most saw their father only at the dinner table. A number never saw their father for days at a time. The average time father and son were alone together for an entire week was seven and a fraction minutes.

Laughing

If I were starting my family again, I would laugh more. I see now that I was much too serious. While my children loved to laugh, I often must have conveyed the idea that being a parent was painful.

I remember when I laughed with my children—at the humorous plays they put on for the family, at the funny stories shared from school, at the times I fell for their tricks and catch questions. I recall the squeals of delight when I laughed with them and shared in their stunts on the lawn or living-room floor. And I remember the times they told of these experiences with joyful expressions, years later. When I laughed with my children, our love was enlarged and the door was open for doing many other things together.

Like most important experiences in life, none of these are great ideas or difficult to remember. These simple suggestions, however, can make relationships with our children more meaningful and shape the future of a child more than great things which demand a great deal of money or exceptional ingenuity. Somehow we manage enough muscle to handle the big things of life but forget that life is largely made up of little things. So a father's faithfulness in the small things of life determines to a great degree the happiness of the home. ●

Dad's Night at Home

by Don Crawford

"You really don't mind taking care of the boys while I go to the Ladies' Aid picnic, do you?" my wife asked one day last summer.

"No, no, of course not," I answered.

"Your supper is in the refrigerator. Be sure the children get to bed on time. Timmy should be in bed by six—he didn't take his nap . . . and the other boys by seven."

"Sure, sure," I said. "You go on—and have fun." It wasn't yet five. I'd have time to wash the car.

I took Tim's playpen outside and put him in it. The six- and the four-year-old followed me to the car. "We want to help you, Daddy," Garry said. Four-year-old Doug nodded agreement. I filled a pail with water and gave each boy a cloth. "You work on that side of the car."

I'd nearly finished my side when Tim started fussing, so I decided I'd better feed him.

As I started toward him I heard the sound of running water. I turned—Doug, who had discovered how the gas cap opened, was about to "fill 'er up" with the water hose. I grabbed him just in time and was explaining why he should never, never play with Daddy's gas cap, when I saw the mud streaks on the door.

"Dougie dropped his cloth in the dirt," Gary explained.

I looked at the muddy water which Gary was using to "clean" the chrome and suggested they each get a clean rag—a very dry one—to "polish it up good."

After Tim's meal I realized why Rita always bathed him after he ate. At 6:20 when Tim was abed, I called the boys. I noticed mud on Doug's clothes. "I falled down in the water," he said.

By 6:40 supper was ready and I wasn't too far behind schedule.

After the meal I had the boys take their baths while I went out to investigate.

The top of the car wasn't bad. What bothered me were the mud streaks *all over the side of the car I'd already cleaned.*

By 7:30 the boys were ready for bed.

I sat down wearily and the boys climbed on my lap, each holding his own devotional book. I quickly read the stories and reviewed each boy's Bible verse. "Now to bed," I said.

"But, Daddy," said the four-year-old. "I wanna tell Jesus—"

"It's late already," I told him.

"We always talk to Jesus before we go to bed," Gary reminded me. Doug was apparently anxious to tell Jesus something, and when I saw the glow on his face, I assented.

"Dear Jesus," he said with delight, "I helped Daddy wash the car today!"

Rags to Riches

by Robert L. Niklaus

Henry Turnidge at the age of 22 was a figure of broken strength. His sturdy frame, tanned and toughened by years of felling timber, convulsed with sobs. Hot tears disappeared in the sawdust of his deserted, bankrupt sawmill in Monroe, Oregon. Rough, calloused hands crumbled three separate letters, all bearing the same message from impatient creditors: "Pay up or we sue."

As he sobbed, a strange new thought elbowed into his mind. "Why don't you let me help you? I'm your Father. You're my son."

The force of this thought arrested his anguish. Father and son! "In my five years as a Christian I had never seen that," remembers Turnidge today. "I had read it but it never dawned on me. God was my Father, and I had the privilege of asking him for help. For the first time in my life I said from my heart, 'Father.' That's all."

In that sacred moment back in 1921, the young man made promises to God that have endured intact over 50 years. Now at the age of 74 Turnidge sees how those promises became guidelines to blessing.

The first thing young Henry did was to make God senior shareholder of his bankrupt sawmill. "I made him a promise: 'I'll take you as my partner. I'll consult you freely on every detail.' "

That decision led him out of the unsuccessful sawmill into a prosperous logging business. Eventually he turned to mint farming and founded an industry for which Willamette Valley, Oregon, is now noted.

"I operated on the principle in James 1:5, 'If any of you lack wisdom, let him ask of God,' " recalls Turnidge. "I'd get an idea of a profitable business deal and ask the Lord to guide me. Then I would start out and do all I could to make that deal. But if complications began to come in, I'd back off. I'd run from it because I saw that God was speaking. How else could he speak? That is really the key to my financial success."

Turnidge's money-making did not begin the day he made the Lord his senior business partner. He had first to eliminate a whopping $10,000 debt incurred at the sawmill. Here again he discovered a guideline to blessing: honesty in money matters with both God and man.

Referring to that bleak day in the sawmill, he remembers, "I went home as happy as if every bill had been paid. I went to bed and for the first time in weeks I really slept. I knew now I had a Father looking after me."

He sold the sawmill to eliminate some debts. Then, with an old team of pulling horses no one would buy, he set out to pay off the remaining bills.

The following morning a lumberman came unexpectedly and offered him a short-term job at 35¢ an hour and $4 per day for the team. "I went over there and did that job and made $35. Afterward I cried for joy. I had made a promise to God that I would give him a tenth. So I sat right down and wrote out a check for $3.50 to my pastor."

The very next day another job contract was offered him. This time he cleared $400. He sent some money to each of his creditors and $40 to his pastor.

This became the pattern for several years. Contracts came in close-order file, one after another. At a time when $125 per month was good wages he never made less than $400. Eventually he paid every bill.

As Henry's logging business boomed, so did his giving to the Lord. Rev. Donald Bubna, at present his pastor in the Christian and Missionary Alliance Church of Salem, Oregon, estimates that over the years Turnidge has put almost one million dollars into the Lord's work.

Henry agrees to this estimate, but adds, "I don't know where it came from. I kept my vow to tithe right straight through. A long time ago I raised my giving to 20 percent, then 30, and finally 50 percent. Still it seems that the Lord just opens up opportunities one right after another. I don't know where the money came from, but I have tried to pass it on."

Another lifetime guideline to blessing emerged from those early days of hard times. After finishing one contract with his pulling team in Salem, Henry heard about another job. "I wanted it in the worst way," he admits, "so I went to see the people about the job.

"They told me, 'We're glad you came but there is one man ahead of you.'

"I tried to get it every way I could. I went home and began to scheme how I could cut out that guy ahead of me.

"All at once I discovered I wasn't happy. I forgot to talk to the Lord about that job. And so it just seemed the Lord spoke again to me so definitely, 'I thought you said you were going to make me your senior partner.' It was just that real.

"I said, 'Father, forgive me. From this time on you take that job over. If you want me to have it you just provide the way.' "

Happiness returned to the young logger and he stopped thinking about the tempting job someone else got to before him.

Three days later an old logging buddy dropped in to visit. Henry invited him to lunch and they had a great time joking and swapping stories.

Just before his friend stood to leave, he said, "I think I had better tell you why I came. There's a big logging job—here in Salem. The company said I could have it, but the job is too big for me. I just came over to see if you would be interested in being my partner. We could take it together."

Henry was too stunned to answer. This man, his friend, was that anonymous logger he had been trying to cheat out of the contract.

"That lesson stayed with me all my life," Turnidge says. "When we take God into our business he has a plan for us. But his plan doesn't include conniving."

Since the Lord was senior partner in all Turnidge's business ventures, it became natural for him to witness to all he met in his work. This grew to be an important guideline to blessing.

Even at the age of 74, he still says, "I don't make a deal with a businessman but what I talk to him about the Lord. I have seen bankers right there in the bank sit and cry when I talk about God. They're that hungry."

He recalled one banker notorious for his roughness. Henry made it a point to say a little to him about the Lord each time he went into the bank. One Sunday afternoon a car came careening up the lane to his house. It was the rough banker, drunk but serious. That day Turnidge brought the banker and Jesus Christ together.

He also seeks opportunities to witness to men who work for him. His special concern is for the 40 or 50 transients who work on his mint farm each summer.

Would he have done anything different in his half-century contract with God? "If I had my life to live over again, I'd make a lot of changes, but I don't think I could be any happier than I have been. I'm looking forward to going home to heaven, but I'm still ready to work and am just as happy as can be."

When Henry Turnidge does get to his eternal home, he will see what he always believed: those guidelines for his earthly life have their origin and end in God. ●

Just a Hunk of Junk by Lloyd Mattson

Read 1-11-85

I can remember as clearly as though it had happened this morning. I can still see that molding, weathered chunk of harness with a buckle turned green. How amused I was at the wonder my son found in the ancient sawmill, the tumbling bunkhouse, the barn with the swayback roof where he found the old leather strap.

"Aw, please, Dad. Why can't I keep it?" he asked when I spoke to him about it.

"That's just junk. It smells. Throw it away."

He threw it on a pile of sawdust so old that grass grew on it, then climbed into our station wagon and sat looking through the dusty side window.

More than once I've weighed the percentages of finding that old strap again. I'd keep it on my desk. When I talked to men and boys I'd show it to them and tell them that a boy's values are different from a man's—and how a man looks back and wishes he had understood.

I'm sure my son has forgotten the strap. My sons are men now, or nearly so. Our values grow closer together each year, for now there are grandsons. I am grateful that despite my paternal bumbling my children serve the living Christ. I am grateful too that they are my friends. Yet that old leather strap, and what it symbolizes, haunts me.

Helping a boy become God's man, which is the task of Christian fatherhood, demands miracles. Most dads have some distance to cover in their own personal journey toward full manhood, for manhood is more than the accumulation of years. No unfailing formula exists to guarantee paternal success, but I think there are some principles to guide a man as he pursues the high calling of fatherhood.

One key factor is *time*. Men with no time to play ball with their boys may need to find time later to sit in juvenile court. Men with sons now grown discover that the loss was not to the son only. How many more good memories I could have had! I can't recall what it was that made me so busy.

Recently I visited a friend I had not seen for several years. We laughed as jerky home movies reminded us of past days. I was dumping a pail of mountain trout on the grass at the Box Y Ranch. He was clowning with the camera. And there was his son, fairly bursting with adventure.

"That was the greatest week of our lives," my friend said. "We have relived it again and again. It made a difference between me and my boy."

The difference in time—time spent with a boy in a world of boy values, boy laughter, boy discoveries, boy dreams, boy wonder. Boy things like an old leather strap.

A second principle for helping boys toward manhood involves *listening*. Listening acknowledges the importance of a person. Half-listening is an affront, and children know when you are half-listening. Remember how you listened for that first word? But how soon we close our ears.

The real satisfaction of adventure is in sharing it. That hole-in-one, or tackle-busting trout—what good are they if there is no friend at hand to tell? A child bursting with juvenile trivia is easily turned off. Sometimes permanently.

The child need not command instant attention whenever the whim to talk possesses him. But there are magic moments when you can give no greater gift than listening.

A painful principle of growth depends on *trust*. There comes the time when a boy must test his wings. Probably he will fail. Maybe he must. How do you know whether you can fly if you are never allowed to try? Sooner or later Dad must turn over the car keys. Trusting is not wanton permissiveness. Youth wants boundaries, but growing up compels a boy to extend his area of self-determination.

Trust is not trust where there is no risk. Wrong choices may be made, but no error of judgment should cut off communication. The uncertainties of growing up often cloud a boy's judgment, but too often Dad's pride becomes the issue rather than the lad's welfare.

The most elusive of all the good-father traits is *honesty*. A lad said to me, "If just *once* my dad would admit he was wrong!" Why does this I-must-be-right demon possess us? Why do I go to such lengths to justify some boner? Why is it so impossible to say, "I'm sorry"?

Consider the family car. What tempests arise when it comes home with a wrinkled fender! (Unless Dad was driving, then all manner of reasons fly why said wrinkle was, if not another's fault, an unavoidable accident.) Must the agony of facing Father be heaped upon the pain of police reports? Blessed is the home where a fallible father first wrinkles the fender.

The fruit of honesty and humility is a climate of confidence. How tight the rein? How long? This is every father's dilemma. Prayer and patience can produce a wisdom beyond the unaided capability of the man who is still growing toward maturity along with his son.

Embracing all principles for fatherhood is *love*. Love that laughs and cries, that praises and spanks, love that spreads its mystic aura even when sons rebel. Mothers can kiss a son good-bye as he leaves for college, but dads must shake hands. Yet there must never be a moment when the son doubts Dad's love.

One August night in the high Cascades a boy knit together this whole matter. That night we had filled the mountain air with jovial song, clusters of men and boys sharing a late-night lunch. In a flash, joy turned to terror with the cry of a boy on fire. A lantern flamed, a form writhed on the ground, clawing dust to his face. Boys and men smothered flames.

Bill's command of himself spared him tragedy. By hurling himself to the dust he had extinguished the flames about his face before severe harm could be done. There would be some pain, but no need to carry him nine difficult miles over a mountain pass for medical aid.

Bill shared a long night with his father in their tent. When morning came the father tenderly washed and dressed the blistered chest and neck. He carried food to his son. By noon, Bill had rejoined the campers, and now, in the last moments of our closing campfire, Bill spoke:

"Last night I couldn't sleep much. I sort of . . . hurt. I kept asking God, 'Why me? Why should I get hurt?' I got some answers. I settled some things with God. There's something else. Before last night I wasn't really sure my dad cared about me. You know how it is. I wasn't really sure. *But now I know.*"

A touch. A smile. Maybe a listening ear. A boy must never be left to wonder if Dad really loves him.

Got any "hunks of junk" you should cherish for your children's sake? ●

The Long Dinner

by Christopher Auer

Read 1-12-85

I guess every family has its ups and downs. One of our definite downs was what my family calls "The Long Dinner."

It started innocently enough with meat loaf as the main course, and the promise of my mother's fantastic chocolate cake for dessert. My behavior hadn't been too bad that day, so it looked like I'd get my piece of cake easy. But when I sat down at the table I realized I had a big problem to deal with: Brussels sprouts.

I don't think there's anything in the whole world more disgusting than Brussels sprouts. How anyone can eat a green vegetable that smells like garbage is beyond me. Too bad for me, they're my father's favorite! Also too bad for me is my father's rule that we have to eat a little bit of everything that's on the table.

My first plan was to ignore them, but halfway through the meal my father noticed I hadn't taken any.

"How about some Brussels sprouts, Sport?" he asked.

"I don't care for any tonight, thank you," I calmly replied.

He just smiled at me and then, *plop,* deposited three of them on my plate. So much for ignoring them, I thought.

I was mad. There was no way I was going to eat them. No way. I'd had a rough enough day as it was. But I couldn't think how to get rid of them. Just then, my little brother flipped a bowl of mashed potatoes upside down on his head. That kid has problems, I said to myself, but I saw my chance and quickly slipped one of the Brussels sprouts back into its bowl. One down and two to go.

To get rid of the second one, I decided on a riskier course.

"Dad," I said, "What are bosoms?"

As my father coughed and turned red, I palmed the second sprout and snuck it into the arrangement of dried flowers at the center of the table.

"Have you been playing with Petey Perkins again?" he asked.

"No!" I answered.

"We'll talk about it later," he said.

My vision of chocolate cake began to fade when I finished my roll and realized the only thing left on my plate was the third Brussels sprout, and I was fresh out of ways to dispose of it. I was even thinking of eating it when my dog Max nudged my leg. That cake was as good as mine. Using my napkin, I slowly slipped the sprout onto my lap, where Max greedily devoured it. I won!

"May I help clear the table?" I asked.

"It's your turn anyway, creepo," said Meg.

I smiled at her, knowing that in half an hour she was going to get the worst lump of her life.

"What's the matter with Max?" my mother asked suddenly.

Max braced himself in the corner, wheezing like our old station wagon on cold mornings. I knew it! The Brussels sprout had killed Max!

"I think there's something caught in his throat," said my father, stepping close to him. "Spit it out, Max; spit it out!"

Max spat it out. It was the Brussels sprout.

Max growled at the vegetable and then looked at me like he was terribly, terribly hurt.

"You don't suppose he took it out of the bowl or something when we weren't looking, do you?"

"I'd be more inclined to believe the 'or something,' " said my father, "and I'd be willing to bet on the 'we weren't looking' part."

"Daddy, do I have to sit here and look at what Max spit up?" complained Meg.

"No," he replied. "You can clean it up."

"That's not fair!" she cried.

"And while you're at it, young lady, you can pick up the one you 'accidentally' dropped under Ben's high chair."

Meg shut her mouth and did as she was told. My father was getting that tone in his voice like the time I blew up his bowling ball with my chemistry set.

"Meanwhile," he went on, looking at me, "I'm sure you'd be more than happy to serve each of you another Brussels sprout."

As I miserably carried out his orders, I vainly hoped for a policeman to ring our doorbell and arrest my father for child abuse. I looked to my mother for help.

"No cake until you eat it," she said.

I hate it when they team up like that. I looked over at Meg. She wasn't making any moves to eat hers, either.

"I have an announcement to make," I said loudly. Everyone looked at me. My mother came back in from the kitchen. "I am never, and I mean never, going to eat another Brussels sprout again, including this one." With that, I folded my arms across my chest and sat back in my chair. There was a long pause.

"I also have an announcement to make," said my father as he leaned menacingly toward me, stopping an inch in front of my face. "You're not only going to eat that Brussels sprout, you'll eat Brussels sprouts for breakfast, lunch, and dinner, if I say so, until you're 18! Is that understood?" This last statement was not only very loud, but was punctuated by his pounding on the table which knocked over his glass of milk. The spilt milk rushed toward him and cascaded off the edge of the table onto his lap. He let out a yell and jumped straight up, hitting his head on the chandelier and his funny bone on the way down, then hopped around the room howling, "Ooo! Ooo! Ooo!"

My father's anger terrified Meg, who gulped down her Brussels sprout and bolted from the dining room. I never could count on her for support.

Five minutes later, my father (in a clean pair of pants) was back at the table eating his cake. "Mmm. The best you've ever made, Barb," he said to my mother.

I followed his fork as he took another mouthful, then another. It was too much for me. I burst into tears.

"Please, please, please, let me have some!" I begged.

My father studied me for several seconds. "You know the rules," he finally said. "You'll sit here, young man, until that vegetable is eaten. I don't care if it takes all week!" Throwing his napkin down, he stormed out of the room, and I collapsed on the table sobbing.

When I awoke, it was dark. The table had been cleared except, of course, for my plate. I heard my mother and father in the kitchen.

"This is ridiculous, Ted."

"The only thing that's ridiculous is children that rule households."

"Well, you should know."

With that, my father came into the dining room.

"Hello," he said, sitting down next to me.

He took off his glasses and rubbed his eyes. He continued as he put them back on. "Please try to understand my position as head of this household. If you don't eat this Brussels sprout, then next week Meg won't do her homework. In a couple of years Ben won't go to school at all! Meg will marry a lion tamer or something! You'll all forget to vote, and then, presto! Before you know it, some Russian kid who right now is eating his Brussels sprouts will march into our nation's capital, kick the President out on the street, and declare himself our dictator! Do you want that to happen? *Do you?*"

I slunk down in my chair.

The hope of the world was a smelly, cold Brussels sprout on my plate.

"Ted," my mother interrupted, "I'm making my shopping list and need to know what you would like for dinner tomorrow."

Father sighed. "What are my choices?"

"Liver and bacon, or liver with cream sauce."

His eyes narrowed and his hands went to his hips. "You know very well," he said at last, "that you agreed never to serve that to me again."

"I don't remember that."

For some reason, what my mother said had a strange effect on my father. He paced the floor. He sat down, then got up and looked out the window. He adjusted the drapes. Cautiously he sat down again.

"I'll make an agreement with you," he said. "I promise that you will never have to eat Brussels sprouts again."

"Never?" I asked.

"Never," he said.

There was an uncomfortable pause.

"I have to eat this one though, don't I," I said.

"Yes, you do," was the answer.

"May I eat it any way I want?" I asked.

"Within reason," he replied.

It wasn't a complete victory, but like my father says, sometimes you have to lose a battle in order to win a war. I lost the battle with the help of an entire bottle of ketchup and a half gallon of chocolate milk.

The less said, the better. At the end of an hour, my piece of cake was before me at last. I unfortunately could not even take one bite of it.

I guess that's what they mean by, "You can't have your cake and eat it, too." ●

How's Your Image, Dad?

by Paul Anderson

The biggest problem our young people face today is not drug abuse, political radicalism, a promiscuous society, or even atheism.

I'm convinced the greatest problem confronting today's youth is the lack of strong leadership in the home. For without this God-ordained leadership, there is little protection against outside evils.

Every home needs a man who is willing to run things.

I don't say this as a super male chauvinist. Rather, as the substitute father for hundreds of youths over the past 13 years. I have yet to encounter a young person in trouble whose difficulty could not be traced to the lack of a strong father-image in the home.

Either the father was absent from the home, or he had lost his position as family leader.

Our liberal society—in undermining the basic concept of marriage, advancing unbiblical feminist viewpoints, and ridiculing male authority—has effectively eroded the traditional father-image.

Take, for example, the numerous situation comedies on television where Father is the family idiot. Or look at the commercials, where Father is often the goat of the household. Or the cartoons, comic strips, books, movies, you-name-it in which Father is depicted as the bungling mismanager.

It's all too easy for Dad to slip into the mold that society has shaped for him and abandon his responsibilities. The result of this attitude is increasingly evident in our juvenile courts. Without adequate leadership, our children have lost a vital feeling of security.

If a young man has no leadership in his home, he is not going to respond to authority anywhere else. Nor is he going to become a good leader in his own home or work, and certainly it will be difficult for him to submit to God's will.

If a young lady does not have a worthy father to relate to, she is not going to become a good wife or mother.

You don't have to take my word for it. Psychiatrists and family counselors have plenty of statistics to prove the need of a guiding father-image for a happy life.

In most cases, the only person who can provide a healthy father-image in the home is you, Dad.

Your leadership is more important to your family than the material comforts you supply. The father who tries to give his family everything is not necessarily a good father—particularly if he withholds leadership and love.

To me, a good father is a man who constantly tries to lead his family in the right direction. He says what he means—and means what he says.

Yes, you may make mistakes. We all do, but this is no excuse to quit. I'm glad my father didn't. I used to worry about him. What a dumb father, I thought. I was sure at one time that I was adopted. But I finally woke up to the fact that he was guiding me in the best way he knew—and that *I* didn't know it all.

I've made plenty of my own mistakes. Not long ago I was sitting watching TV when my five-year-old daughter came up and said, "Daddy, see if I still fit." She wanted to see if I could still hold her like a baby.

I nearly cried when I put her on my lap because her feet almost touched the ground. Where had the time gone? Why hadn't I done more with her, taken her places, spent more time with her?

I felt guilty for the stretches I had to be away from home to make money for our tribe of neglected kids. But I realized I had made the only decision I could, for in so doing I also shared the Good News of Christ.

It is important to remember that what God has called you to do, he'll help you accomplish. And he'll bless your sincere effort. God's promise to both follower and leader is spelled out in Scripture:

"Children, obey your parents in the Lord. . . . Fathers, provoke not your children to wrath: but bring them up in the nurture and admonition of the Lord. . . . Knowing that whatsoever good thing any man doeth, the same shall he receive of the Lord" (Eph. 6:1, 4, 8).

The only way a man can lead his family in the right direction is by always seeking the divine guidance of God's Holy Spirit. He can't do it alone.

I thought I was on top of the world when I was acclaimed the world champion weightlifter at the 1956 Olympics in Melbourne. But I've come to realize I couldn't lift a finger without God's enabling.

The biggest thrill in my life is serving Christ. My greatest opportunity is not in lifting more than any other human, but in being the kind of leader God would have me be for my wife, Glenda, our daughter, and the more than 350 boys at the Paul Anderson Youth Home in Vidalia, Ga., and its twin in Dallas, Tex.

It was within this larger "family" that my need for God's constant help was brought home to me not long ago. Like other fathers, I felt I should attend the football games the boys from our home played as members of the local high school squad. One of our boys, Danny, was the team captain, and an all-state tackle.

One Friday evening when I had been away giving a series of talks, I arrived in Vidalia two hours before gametime—for a contest 100 miles away. After grabbing a bite to eat I drove on to the game with two of my staff members.

Just before the first half ended I noticed something was wrong with Danny. He was staggering back to the huddle when he collapsed. I went down onto the field.

"We need to get him into a hospital," the doctor who had gone to Danny's aid was saying. "It looks like a brain injury." We took Danny to the Macon, Ga., General Hospital, where the neurosurgeon located a large blood clot on the boy's brain. He prepared to operate—and we began the long vigil.

The responsibility of being a father rested heavily upon me during the four-hour operation. I did the only thing I could. I turned Danny over to the Lord.

The operation over, the doctor reported only that Danny had a chance to live. The members of my staff urged me to go home, but I shook my head.

God not only gave me the strength to stay with Danny all that night, he also strengthened Danny. Four days after surgery the neurosurgeon announced, "I can't understand it, but Danny has completely recovered. I see no reason why he can't live a completely normal life again in a few more weeks."

Just a week after the injury Danny was back in school. That night he was present on the field, dressed in his uniform, as one of the largest crowds in history packed the Vidalia High School stadium.

His head shaved and bandaged, Danny walked out on the field. As captain of his team, he shook hands with the opposing captain and made the opening decision for his school. It was a lesson to me in the responsibility of leadership.

But a bigger thrill came several months later when God gave me the privilege of seeing Danny walk to the front of our church and publicly acknowledge Jesus Christ as his personal Savior. The best thing I could ever do for Danny, as his substitute father, was to lead him in God's direction.

This is the only sure course you can take, Dad, in your role as family leader. It's the only hope for our homes, I'm convinced. Real strength is spiritual, and it's available to all in Jesus Christ. ●

When You Lose Your Job

by Brian Dyck

Two years ago my wife and I returned to British Columbia from Oregon to find employment. I had spent eight years in university training for a profession. Although I had a temporary job when I first moved to Victoria, I was unable to find stable employment. My unemployment was a time of testing.

At times I became frustrated and had doubts about the future. Other times I felt self-pity and implored, "Why me?" However, I also experienced a great deal of support and prayers from family, friends, and people in our church.

After five months of seeking employment, God answered our prayers and provided me with a job related specifically to my training. While the experience of each unemployed individual would be different, it might be helpful to suggest some ways of coping with the problem.

The concept of work as a divinely instituted element of human existence is rooted in God's creation (Gen. 2:2). In his book, *In Praise of Leisure*, Harold Lehman indicates that work not only provides the basic necessities of life, but it also helps to maintain a standard of living, satisfy psychological needs, promise future benefits, and supply moral satisfactions.

The Bible warns about the consequences of laziness and idleness (Prov. 6:9-11; 2 Thess. 3:10-11). Although Scripture says little directly related to unemployment, it does provide some principles for handling disappointments and hardships.

Recognize God's control. For many people, unemployment brings the feeling that things are out of control.

The Bible reminds us that God is in control of the universe, nations, and the lives of individual people. One example of this is indicated in the book of Job. The first major loss that Job suffered was his business (Job 1:13-17). Later virtually everything he had was taken away.

While Satan was the instigator of these misfortunes, God specified the limits. Job's specific situation may not be directly applicable to being unemployed today, but I think several things from the book could be applied in viewing the unemployment situation.

First, we may not understand the things that happen to us, especially when they first occur. In some cases, we may be able to change the circumstances that affect us; in other cases this may not be possible. But it is important to remember God is concerned about us and knows our needs (1 Pet. 4:7; Matt. 6:8), and things are ultimately governed by God, not man.

Second, unemployment can provide an opportunity for spiritual growth. Such growth usually involves a refining process. Job says, "But he knows the way I take; when he has tested me, I will come forth as gold" (Job 23:10). Near the end of the book we find that he not only recognizes God's omnipotence (42:2), but he also prays for his friends who had rebuked him (42:7-10).

In facing unemployment, God may teach us patience. We may also learn to become more dependent on God and to more fully accept God's control over our lives.

Commit it to God. The psalmist says, "Commit thy way unto the Lord; trust also in him and he shall bring it to pass" (Ps. 37:5).

One way we can commit our situation to God is through prayer. It allows us to draw close to God and to remind him of our situation, even though he is already aware of it. The Scriptures indicate we are to pray persistently (Luke 11:8; 18:1) and with thanksgiving (Phil. 4:6-7). By drawing near to him in prayer, we are able to draw upon a strength that is greater than ours and receive the peace that he promised us through his Son.

A second way we can commit our unemployment to God is through reading the Bible. From it we learn about God's character and the experiences of others who seemed to face unsolvable problems, but who saw these problems resolved because they trusted God. We also are given hope for the future and strength to cope with each day.

Fellowship with others. The Bible instructs us to bear one another's burdens or problems (Gal. 6:2). Two types of fellowship that were particularly helpful to me were a Bible study group and a men's prayer breakfast.

Through these types of fellowship I became aware that other people had faced or were confronting the same problem. It also allowed me to share my concern for employment and to identify specific prayer requests. I further received a great deal of support and encouragement. They accepted me for who I was regardless of my employment status.

Practical steps. In my situation, one of the beginning steps was to develop a resumé. Bookstores usually carry books which contain many different examples. It is important to adequately and truthfully represent yourself. The resumé, in applying for some jobs, is the only picture a prospective employer might have of you. I slightly modified my resumé depending on the job that I was applying for.

I further checked various information sources, such as newspaper, government offices, and various ads, usually on a daily basis. The source of information about my present job was a government office. Most people at such offices can also provide additional suggestions about job opportunities.

Psychologist Gary Collins, in his book, *Relax and Live Longer,* suggests that physical activity can be helpful for coping with various pressures of life. I found playing racquetball and jogging particularly helpful. In other situations, writing, reading, tinkering, doing house maintenance or volunteer work can provide a beneficial way of dealing with the new abundance of time thrust on an unemployed individual.

Unemployment usually influences our lifestyles. In some cases, this may require certain changes in our daily habits. Such things as coupon clipping, clever sewing ideas, and economical cooking can help to stretch limited dollars.

Coping with unemployment is not easy. The way we view this experience, however, can either produce bitterness or growth. It's a clear choice for those who really want to work for good pay! ●

My Graduation Gift

by Bernard Pearson

Dad clutched the letter he had taken out of the mailbox and wondered what the answer would be. As he walked slowly up the driveway, many thoughts came to mind. He thought of the time some 25 years earlier when he had bidden his folks farewell in Sweden and set forth for the land of opportunity in America. He thought of early years in this country, working in lumber camps and sawmills, all the time saving from his small salary for the time when he could use it to make a down payment on a parcel of land of his own.

He remembered how his dream had come true in the purchase of 100 acres of unimproved land. He thought of the work which had gone into breaking it up into fields, clearing the brush, woods, and rocks. He thought of the house, barn, and buildings he had built from lumber cut from the land. He thought of the good wife he had wooed, and won, and without whose help he could never have made a go of it.

He reminisced on the eight children born to them. He thought of the hardships which had come and gone—that first winter when he had nearly died in his wife's arms as the wolves howled in the swamps nearby. He thought of that first herd of cattle that he lost from tuberculosis, when there were no indemnities or help of any kind. He thought also of the fine herd he had since acquired. He thought of the fire which had destroyed the barn and outbuildings when he had little insurance. He looked around and saw the beautiful trees which had grown from seed his mother had brought from Sweden when he had sent for her there.

He looked up and breathed a prayer, "O God, if it please You, let me keep this farm."

The letter in Dad's hand carried an answer from the mortgage company. Would it grant an extension on his loan? This was in the early 1930s. The depression was at its worst. To top it off, there had been a dry summer in this part of Minnesota. When autumn came, and with it the due date on the mortgage, there just wasn't money to pay it. Dad had written asking an extension for 90 days.

When he reached the house we all crowded around to hear the verdict. He read the letter slowly to himself, then asked one of us to read it. *"If you can pay it in 90 days,"* it said, *"you can pay it now. If you don't, we will take your place."*

Dad looked at Mom. She looked at him. He then said, "Well, I guess they will just have to take it." Mom didn't say anything. She just went to her bedroom and stayed for a long time, so long in fact that we were beginning to be worried about her. Then she came out and through her tears sang the old Swedish hymn, *"Though He giveth and He taketh, He His children ne'er forsaketh."*

It seemed no time till Thanksgiving. We youngsters were always pestering Mom about what we would have for dinner on that special day. She said, "Oh, we'll have something good." In her heart I am sure she was at her wit's end. Finally, the day before Thanksgiving she called the boys together and asked us to go out and shoot some squirrels. We couldn't get too enthusiastic about it, but we did as she asked. This she made into a huge meat pie with vegetables. When dinner came we all sat down around our big table and Dad asked the blessing.

What a prayer he prayed that day! He thanked the Lord for his family, for their sound minds and bodies, for our food when so many around the world had none, for our wonderful country, for our farm of which we still had possession, and asked God in His mercy that He would help us to be able to keep it.

Then, we went after that food. How good that meat pie was! No steak prepared by a world-famous chef could compare to our meal that day. There was laughter to make all the troubles pass off into the distance.

Christmas came and with it our preparations for the holiday. We always celebrated Christmas in the Swedish custom of a feast on Christmas Eve, after which gifts would be exchanged around the Christmas tree. What should a boy buy for five brothers, two sisters, Mom and Dad as well as an aunt who made her home with us, when he had only ten cents?

I racked my brains and finally bought each one a penny candy bar (they were big in those days). I wrapped them all individually and put them under the tree. There were made-over clothes and toys also under the tree.

After the chores were done we gathered in the front room and all the children gave the pieces they had learned for the Sunday school program, after which we sang carols. Dad took down the Bible and read the old Christmas story, after which he prayed, thanking God for sending his Son to give us life through him.

Then, the presents. Mom gave us each a huge gingerbread—a boy for the boys and a girl for the girls. My sister had bought us each a cup that said sister for her sisters and brother for her brothers. In her hurry she had miscounted and I got a card saying, "You will get yours later."

Talk about fun, we had it! We laughed till we cried and Mom and Dad had to get harsh to finally get us to bed.

That winter was unusually cold. Twenty and 30 below zero were common. For a boy who had to walk four miles to school each day it seemed never to end. Dad now had begun efforts to have the mortgage refinanced. This proved to be successful and the means of saving the farm. Times were difficult. There was a continual struggle for survival, but at last graduation time came and I was to finish high school. Dad borrowed our neighbor's old Model T Ford so we could all go to the graduation. I sat on the platform that night, thankful that I had put forth the effort to be an honor student, when I looked down and saw Mom and Dad sitting there in their best clothes, watching the proceeding with quiet interest.

Later that evening, when we were home and I was going to bed, Mom called me aside, looked at me with tears in her eyes and said, "Dad and I feel so bad that we don't have any present to give you."

Nothing to give me? I wonder how many other graduates had received anything like the wonderful gifts my parents had given me! ●

Fathers Can Be Beautiful!

by Marcia Schwartz

High on the neighbor's roof on a fine, crisp October morning, I saw a beautiful thing. There they were: a roofer and his three sons slapping on green shingles in the bright morning sun. The breeze wisped their blond hair from stocking caps and sweatshirt hoods.

The three boys, between ten and sixteen years of age, maneuvered agilely in sneakers about the roof, sometimes boosting themselves along in a sitting position on well-patched jeans. The oldest boy lined up the shingles, deftly placed a nail from his apron and with several sharp blows of the hammer anchored it in place. The second boy carried shingles to his father, who cut them with swift precision and drilled them to the roof with a hammer-gun.

The smallest boy scooted up and down the ladder gathering up scraps on the roof and in the yard below, his white sweatshirt striking as a dove against the blue sky and lofty green of the neighboring pines. The ring of their hammers and the slap of the shingles reverberated through the whole outdoors. Each was a "fiddler" of sorts, making his own kind of music on that roof.

And corny as it may sound, my heart was lifted to see them so busily at work. In an age when families are falling apart and the apprenticeship of son to father in learning a trade is outmoded, when manual labor is scorned, and some young people don't know the meaning of work, that strong young father and his sons were indeed *beautiful!*

Then in November, I saw it again, the beauty of another father and two small sons playing football.

"Keep your eyes on the ball and keep running," shouted the father, who spiraled the brown pigskin toward a third-grade boy. The boy caught the ball with a shriek and bounded away from a smaller boy, who plodded along behind like a puppy.

"If the opposition catches you, twist out of his grasp"—last words of a father who was besieged by two tugging boys in mud-smeared nylon windbreakers. From the pile of wiggling, twisting males came loud giggles and guffaws. A band of pink in the west didn't light the thinly gray November afternoon, and even a washboard of downy clouds above added little to nature's solemnity, but there in that heap were mirth and warmth and bright lights shining. The most beautiful thing this time was a father and sons at play, a universally simple and natural thing, but paramount to stability—and well-being—and happiness.

Once again I saw a variation of the scene—this time a father held his toddler son in church. The boy's dark head nestled under the chin of the young father, and the stained glass window beyond the pew haloed both their heads with dancing rainbow colors.

"Shh," the father bent to quiet his son and then, impulsively, reacting from an inner conviction, the father grinned and ruffled the bouncy curls of the boy.

My eyes took it in, savoring the moment, the deep, spiritual beauty of a father who loves his offspring and fulfills his role of father to the best of his God-given ability.

"Beauty is truth, truth beauty . . ." said John Keats. And surely it was truth which made each of these scenes so inordinately beautiful for me; the truth and rightness of a father interacting and intertwining his life with his son; a father molding, teaching, caring, just plain involved with his children. The truth of fatherhood at its finest—that's what made each of these scenes so beautiful for me. ●